CONTENTS

S. Hrg. 106–1141

FIRESTONE TIRE RECALL

HEARING

BEFORE THE

COMMITTEE ON COMMERCE, SCIENCE, AND TRANSPORTATION UNITED STATES SENATE

ONE HUNDRED SIXTH CONGRESS

SECOND SESSION

SEPTEMBER 12, 2000

Printed for the use of the Committee on Commerce, Science, and Transportation

U.S. GOVERNMENT PRINTING OFFICE

85–219 PDF WASHINGTON : 2003

For sale by the Superintendent of Documents, U.S. Government Printing Office
Internet: bookstore.gpo.gov Phone: toll free (866) 512–1800; DC area (202) 512–1800
Fax: (202) 512–2250 Mail: Stop SSOP, Washington, DC 20402–0001

SENATE COMMITTEE ON COMMERCE, SCIENCE, AND TRANSPORTATION

ONE HUNDRED SIXTH CONGRESS

SECOND SESSION

JOHN McCAIN, Arizona, *Chairman*

TED STEVENS, Alaska
CONRAD BURNS, Montana
SLADE GORTON, Washington
TRENT LOTT, Mississippi
KAY BAILEY HUTCHISON, Texas
OLYMPIA J. SNOWE, Maine
JOHN ASHCROFT, Missouri
BILL FRIST, Tennessee
SPENCER ABRAHAM, Michigan
SAM BROWNBACK, Kansas

ERNEST F. HOLLINGS, South Carolina
DANIEL K. INOUYE, Hawaii
JOHN D. ROCKEFELLER IV, West Virginia
JOHN F. KERRY, Massachusetts
JOHN B. BREAUX, Louisiana
RICHARD H. BRYAN, Nevada
BYRON L. DORGAN, North Dakota
RON WYDEN, Oregon
MAX CLELAND, Georgia

MARK BUSE, *Republican Staff Director*
ANN CHOINIERE, *Republican General Counsel*
KEVIN D. KAYES, *Democratic Staff Director*
MOSES BOYD, *Democratic Chief Counsel*

FIRESTONE TIRE RECALL

TUESDAY, SEPTEMBER 12, 2000

U.S. SENATE,
COMMITTEE ON COMMERCE, SCIENCE, AND TRANSPORTATION,
Washington, DC.

The Committee met, pursuant to notice, at 9:30 a.m. in room SH–216, Hart Senate Office Building, Hon. John McCain, Chairman of the Committee, presiding.

OPENING STATEMENT OF HON. JOHN McCAIN, U.S. SENATOR FROM ARIZONA

The CHAIRMAN. Good morning. I want to thank the witnesses for their presence this morning. This morning's hearing is important for a variety of reasons. It will offer the committee and the public an opportunity to gain a better understanding of the recall of 14.4 million Firestone tires. More importantly, it will begin the process for this committee and hopefully this Congress to examine and improve the policies of the National Highway Traffic Safety Administration to detect defects and enhance the obligation of industry to provide safe vehicles to consumers.

While a great deal has been said by many people over the past few weeks about this problem, the fact remains that our attention to ensuring the safety of the driving public is fleeting. It unfortunately takes a cumulative tragedy of more than 80 lives to bring our collective attention to the long-overdue task of reforming the way we investigate and remedy vehicle defects.

Let me be clear. It is not my intention to use today's hearings to lay blame upon any individual, company, or Government agency. The liability of the parties involved will be appropriately determined through ongoing investigations and eventually the courts.

The fact is, we all share the blame equally when the system fails. Congress sometimes interferes with Government regulators in the prosecution of their duties, industry can be too focused on profits rather than the safety of the public, and agencies can become bureaucracies more concerned with paperwork than advancing the very causes they were created to serve.

Serious questions remain about what Ford and Firestone knew of this problem and when they knew it. The mounting evidence is making it increasingly difficult to credibly believe that neither of these companies knew anything of this problem until late this summer. A recent *Washington Post* article cites a Firestone report from mid-1998 that shows a dramatic increase in customer claims on one of the tires that is subject to this recall.

Furthermore, annual claims reports from Firestone show an increase in claims associated with the tires subject to the recall beginning in 1996 through 1999. Ford also received numerous complaints about Firestone tires on Explorers in overseas markets. These complaints were significant enough to cause Ford to replace tires in 16 foreign countries.

Taken individually, each of these incidents may not be cause for alarm, but taken collectively it is difficult to believe that no one realized this was a problem until a month ago. Both Ford and Firestone owe the American people an explanation for why it took them so long to act.

I cite this article not as evidence of guilt, but as an example of the problems with the current system. The current system must be changed. When manufacturers fail to tell the truth or purposefully neglect to report safety data, people lose their lives. Severe penalties must result. It is my intention to work with the Ranking Member and other members of the committee to develop legislation to reform the process used to detect, investigate, and recall defective vehicles.

Two weeks ago, I wrote to Secretary Slater about this recall and asked for the administration's recommendations to improve NHTSA's ability to detect defects. I look forward to hearing the Secretary's views on that today.

Additionally, the committee will ask the Inspector General to review the Office of Defects Investigations and make further recommendations on how to improve its functioning and ensure that it has the resources that it needs to protect the public's safety. I am hopeful today we can move beyond recriminations and toward the process of reform.

Again, I want to thank the witnesses for their presence, and I look forward to their testimony.

Senator Hollings.

STATEMENT OF HON. ERNEST F. HOLLINGS, U.S. SENATOR FROM SOUTH CAROLINA

Senator HOLLINGS. First, Mr. Chairman, let me welcome you back to the committee, Senator McCain. We are delighted that you are in good health and back with us.

Let me just sort of file my statement and summarize to save time. What you and I typically have here is a situation where Ford says we ought to recall the Firestone tires, Firestone says we ought to recall the Ford cars, or Explorers. That happens in these lawsuits. I used to try them, and it is like tying two cats by their tails and throwing them over the clothesline and let them claw each other, and that is why we have joint cases and several in the tort procedure, but that is not our duty here.

Our duty here is to try to see how we can improve the situation and facilitate the replacement, if nothing else more than anything else now require the reporting of any overseas recalls. If we had had that, we would have been aware of this at least 2 years ago. Reporting of the lawsuits, there is a *Business Week* article to the effect that the lawyers are at fault. Not at all.

We get into the trial of the case and the other side is ready to settle, and they are ready to pay off, you cannot tell the client that we have got to hold it up because I want to get publicity. The lawyers are not at fault. The company is at fault with all of these lawsuits and taking due diligence. Under that circumstance they should have done something long ago, other than just to recall.

So we ought to have those lawsuits, because when you have a lawsuit it is not just changing a tire, it is damage, probably injury. It could have been life lost. Otherwise, we have got to upgrade the standards. The Firestone tire that is defective that we are talking about complies with the present standard, and so obviously the standards need upgrading, and we need to upgrade the Secretary's budget, because I think we had a severe cutback in the eighties.

We replaced some of that cut, but in contrast the number of automobiles and otherwise to be checked have increased measurably, and so we have got to play a little catch-up on the budget itself.

Thank you very much.

[The prepared statement of Senator Hollings follows:]

PREPARED STATEMENT OF HON. ERNEST F. HOLLINGS, U.S. SENATOR FROM SOUTH CAROLINA

We have convened today to address a very serious issue—a massive number of tires that are alleged to be defective in their design and manufacturing. This matter involves two companies that are giants in their industries: Ford, the number two automaker, and Firestone, the number two tire manufacturer in the world. Firestone, in fact, has a plant in my home state, which is located in Aiken. From the data I have seen almost none of the tires that have been linked to tread separations and accidents have involved tires from that plant.

As I noted, this is a serious case that has yet to be resolved. When the recall was announced on August 9th, it was noted that 46 deaths had been linked to Firestone's tires and Ford's vehicles. Now just a few weeks later, that figure has risen to 88 deaths. Unfortunately, we are still counting.

We have come today to try to get to the bottom of this matter. And there are some important questions that have to be answered. They include:

(1) Is the number of tires that have been designated for recall sufficient or should the recall be extended?

(2) When did the relevant parties—Firestone, Ford and NHTSA—become aware of the problem and did they act appropriately to protect car owners from danger once the problem was discovered?

(3) Are Firestone's tires and Ford's SUVs affected by manufacturing defects and design flaws and have the companies known or should have been aware of these conditions?

But the really crucial question is what is Congress going to do about it? Surely, this case begs for policy changes. Federal tire standards haven't been changed since 1973. Current law allows companies to discover defects and conduct major recalls in foreign countries without having any obligation to inform U.S. regulators or American consumers. The current maximum civil penalties companies face is less than $1 million. How is this going to deter multi-billion dollar companies? Some will criticize NHTSA for not being aggressive enough on the matter. That criticism is warranted. But when the agency went forth with a rule earlier this year to establish updated rollover standards, Members of Congress introduced legislation to block the regulations. In response, I offered language to the State, Justice, Commerce appropriations bill to salvage the rule by deferring the matter to the National Academy of Sciences.

I am currently working with my able chairman on comprehensive legislation to remove the numerous loopholes that exist in today's laws and to ensure DOT has the authority and resources it needs to guard against these egregious actions.

But I also would be remiss if I did not take this time to talk about another policy issue, which I believe is equally important to this case—and that is tort reform. If ever there were a case that proves the fallacy of federal tort reform bills—it's this case. If ever there were a case to prove the foolishness and recklessness of criticisms of trial lawyers—like so many in this body like to do—it's this case. **Eighty-eight deaths** and still counting. These products have been on the market for how long—at least 10 years. And guess who first discovered and exposed the issue? No, it was not members of Congress. No, it was not DOT or Secretary Slater. No, it was not the media, newspapers, nor a Texas television station. It was trial lawyers. They were the individuals who exposed this coverup if there is one. The reason we sit here today testifying before all the media and the nation about this issue is because of the diligent, arduous, persistent work of trial lawyers—those brave men and women lawyers who, unlike their corporate counterparts, work from the sweat of their brow, not on a guarantee but on a contingency fee, in their efforts to seek compensation for those who have suffered a serious injury or loss of a loved one due to a defective product.

I also must point out my aghastness at the aghastness of some members of Congress about this matter. Some act as if this case is something unique. It's not. This conduct happens all the time. Why do you think in the last 5 years there have been over 73 million recalls of automobiles alone?

Have we forgotten the Firestone 500 tire debacle of the late 1970s and early 1980s—**19 million tires recalled on the basis of tread separations, 41 deaths.** And what did the Congress do? It cooperated with the Reagan Administration in slashing NHTSA's budget so it could prevent NHTSA from going after such conduct. Though I have fought years to give NHTSA more FUNDING, and though the Clinton Administration has sought some improvements, the agency has never recovered from the massive budget cuts of that period. **But guess who initiated the review of the Firestone 500 case—plaintiffs' lawyers.**

Have we forgotten the Ford Pinto case involving a defectively designed gas tank that caused Ford Pinto automobiles to explode on impact? Evidence at trial revealed Ford knew the problem existed and could have fixed the gas tank for $11 a car. However, it was not until lawsuits were filed, and a $3.5 million punitive verdict was issued, that the company decided to redesign the car.

Have we forgotten about the GM pickup side-saddle gas tank case—where the company placed a gas tank on the outside of the guard rail causing the vehicle to explode upon impact—resulting in several hundred deaths?

Certainly, I can go on and on, with example after example, but the point is clear that this case we're reviewing today is nothing new. The fact is that most of these matters are exposed and settled through the tort system. Yet, for more than 20 years, members of this body have pushed for the passage of legislation to restrain the tort system from holding companies accountable when they engage in egregious and flagrant conduct. They would do this by making it more difficult for citizens who are injured by such conduct to collect damages from wrongdoers—even in light of evidence that the company concealed information and knew about the dangers of a product before it was marketed. I am often perplexed as to why members of this body would be more enthusiastic about passing legislation to protect Ford and Firestone, even if it's proven they knew of defects in their products, than legislation to give NHTSA more resources to protect the public.

Even as we sit here today, there are product liability, class action and asbestos bills awaiting action. As I mentioned earlier, this case should make it clear as to why it is unwise for Congress to pursue such measures.

The CHAIRMAN. Thank you very much, Senator Hollings.

I would remind my colleagues we have three full panels today, and would respectfully request that their opening statements be as brief as possible.

Senator Hutchison.

STATEMENT OF HON. KAY BAILEY HUTCHISON, U.S. SENATOR FROM TEXAS

Senator HUTCHISON. Thank you, Mr. Chairman. In my home State of Texas alone there are 338,000 Ford Explorers currently registered with the Texas Department of Transportation. I understand from what I have read that the separation on the tires in question is more likely to occur at high temperatures. Well, it is no secret that this summer, Texas has suffered one of the worst droughts in history, and severe high temperature strings, breaking the 100-degree mark most every day of the last 2 months, and so the people of Texas are very concerned about this issue today, and certainly the extent of the danger that is presented in the future.

As the chairman said, we need not to focus so much on the blame, but on what we can do now, and what we can do to prevent anything like this happening in the future, but it is alarming that last week, according to testimony received in the House Commerce Committee, an insurance company investigator notified the agency of NHTSA in July 1998 about the potential defect.

One year later, Ford was offering free replacement tires in Saudi Arabia, Thailand and Malaysia, and yet NHTSA did not begin to look at this situation until May of this year, and by the time the agency commenced a formal investigation in August, at least 41 people had died on American roads, possibly as a result of faulty tires, so I think we need to find out if there is an information gap.

Is there more responsibility that needs to be placed in the hands of NHTSA? We need to know exactly what has happened, and what the time line was, in order to address these issues, which I hope we will be able to do in the hearing today, and then as we go in the future, working on legislation together on a bipartisan basis in Congress.

Thank you, Mr. Chairman.

The CHAIRMAN. Thank you, Senator Hutchison.

Senator Bryan.

STATEMENT OF HON. RICHARD H. BRYAN, U.S. SENATOR FROM NEVADA

Senator BRYAN. Thank you very much, Mr. Chairman, for convening this hearing. I think what we are dealing with this morning is a systemic failure, a failure that has had tragic consequences for 88 Americans who lost their lives and hundreds of others who, as a result of this failure, were injured as a consequence, and for the two companies involved, Ford and Firestone, it is a sordid chapter in the history of two companies that for more than a century have become household names for the American public.

Americans are quite properly indignant when they learn that Firestone initiated and Ford initiated recalls in Saudi Arabia more than year before the notice of recall was issued in this country. Other countries were also given earlier recall notices, Malaysia, Thailand, Venezuela, Colombia, and Ecuador, and the question arises, are not American lives as important to protect and safeguard as lives in these other countries, which were clearly given an earlier notice and opportunity, something that I find particularly troublesome, Mr. Chairman, and perhaps we can get into that issue this morning.

I know nothing about the case that appears on the front page of *The New York Times* dealing with what is called a thick film ignition, a TFI module, but I do know that the language that the courts used in indicting and condemning the actions of Ford are quite troublesome.

Let me just read very briefly. Among the things the court had to say is that Ford's dissimilation reached its nadir in the testimony of Bob Weeks, Ford's witness designated as the most knowledgeable about safety issues, when he insisted that safe is too subjective, and denied knowledge of any written definition of what is safe with Ford Motor Company, and then the court went on to say, rather, it seems Ford used the tortured interpretations of common language to avoid its responsibility to NHTSA, the Environmental Protection Agency, and the consuming public.

Now, I do not know if this is a part of a pattern of conduct or not, but that is something that clearly we need to explore this morning.

And finally, Mr. Chairman, it seems to me we need to examine whether or not NHTSA itself has the tools to do the job, among those things we need to consider is whether or not we ought to increase the amount of civil penalties, whether or not there should be a requirement, and I would think the answer to this is clear, that there ought to be a requirement(s) that a foreign recall require and trigger automatically a notice to the agency that is responsible, NHTSA. That apparently is not the current law. Whether or not the retention of records should be extended for a period of time so that retrospectively we can examine the safety examination as it relates to a product that is later recalled, whether or not the statute of limitations ought to be issued, and whether or not we ought to be amending the statute of limitations on the period of time for reporting defects.

I look forward to hearing from the distinguished panels you have convened this morning, and hopefully we can provide answers this morning to the question that the American public is asking each of us, why were we not given notice much earlier in light of the overwhelming evidence that there was a problem with these tires.

I thank you, Mr. Chairman.

The CHAIRMAN. Thank you. Senator Abraham.

STATEMENT OF HON. SPENCER ABRAHAM, U.S. SENATOR FROM MICHIGAN

Senator ABRAHAM. Thank you, Mr. Chairman. I want to commend you for calling this hearing, and I look forward to working with you both on the hearing today and the legislation you mentioned to ensure that the committee gathers all the facts and provides consumers as much information as we can on the issue of defective tires.

Clearly, I think this hearing should focus on the current tire recall, what should have been done, what should still be done, and what steps in the future must be taken to ensure consumer confidence as well as minimize consumer risk and I think, Mr. Chairman, if we proceed in a constructive and informative fashion we can move closer to answering those important questions.

Also, Mr. Chairman, I would like to just welcome today one of my constituents, Jack Nasser of Ford Motor Company to the Senate Commerce Committee. During his brief tenure as the head of Ford he has built a strong reputation as both a respected business and community leader, and I commend him for both being here today and for what Ford has already launched in an effort to address this problem, but obviously, Mr. Chairman, as a Senator from Michigan I also represent a considerable number of Ford employees in addition to Mr. Nasser, and I would note that they are extremely hardworking and decent craftsmen and women who take great pride in the product they produce.

As the son of a United autoworker myself, I can assure the committee that our auto workers and auto companies are dedicated to providing consumers with the highest quality and safest vehicles possible.

Mr. Chairman, it strikes me that there are several areas of inquiry that we must examine in today's hearing. One, we need to evaluate and understand the circumstances, the reasons that recalls were instituted in other countries and why no similar action took place here in the United States. Second, we must explore the magnitude of the existing recall. Is it sufficient? What are the critical next steps that these companies as well as the Government should take to address the situation, and third, I believe the committee must examine the current Government procedures and practices in addressing this type of situation. Should existing laws and regulations be amended? Are there new steps we should pursue?

I appreciate you taking this step to begin the process in putting the hearing together, and the witness' willingness to be here with us today, and I look forward to working with you, Mr. Chairman, and our colleagues on the committee to address these problems with you.

The CHAIRMAN. Thank you.

Senator Wyden.

STATEMENT OF HON. RON WYDEN, U.S. SENATOR FROM OREGON

Senator WYDEN. Thank you, Mr. Chairman. I will be brief, and really have only three points. The first is, after all that is already on the record I believe that it is thoroughly unreasonable for Firestone to not admit that there is a safety defect after all of these deaths that have been linked to their product.

I think it is also unreasonable that they have failed to disclose the 100 lawsuits, in not reporting to regulators that there were problems. That is point number 1.

Point number 2, as of last week only about a quarter of the recalled Firestone tires had been replaced. Consumers in my home State of Oregon are in the last group of customers under Firestone's phase 3 recall. They are going to have to wait until next year to get replacement tires. I have got a Ford Explorer in the basement of this building, and I will just go through the process in terms of replacement there, but I want to see my constituents get some assistance.

And finally, the last point I want to make, Mr. Chairman, is that today we are going to have witnesses. They are going to be subjected to vigorous questioning, and there will be debate among our colleagues as to what to do, but I would submit that because there were similar hearings 20 years ago with the same company the real challenge now is to ensure that changes are adopted, substantive changes are adopted so that another committee is not sitting in this same room 20 years from now going over the very same issues.

So we ought to recognize that this is our first and foremost challenge today, and I look forward to working with the chairman and our colleagues to addressing this issue, and I thank you.

The CHAIRMAN. Thank you. Senator Burns.

STATEMENT OF HON. CONRAD BURNS, U.S. SENATOR FROM MONTANA

Senator BURNS. Thank you very much, Mr. Chairman. My statement will be very brief. Thank you for calling this hearing, and I think we are fulfilling our oversight responsibility today not just by looking at the continuing stories of this situation, but also at our ability to assure that Government is fulfilling its responsibilities.

Gaps have been noted, if you read the press and what is happening in hearings previous to this one. I think now that probably more gaps will be noted as a result of this hearing. We can take that information, connect the dots, and fill in some of the blanks. The consuming public expects no less.

I look forward to the testimony we will hear today and the questions and answers that will follow these opening statements, and I thank the chairman for convening this hearing.

The CHAIRMAN. Thank you.

Senator Cleland.

STATEMENT OF HON. MAX CLELAND, U.S. SENATOR FROM GEORGIA

Senator CLELAND. Thank you, Mr. Chairman. Welcome back, Mr. Chairman. It is good to see you, Mr. Chairman. Based on what I have heard about these tires, it is a good thing I do not have them on my wheelchair, otherwise I would not be here, probably.

Let me just say that I do recall that, as a student of American history that Henry Ford and Harvey Firestone and Thomas Edison worked closely together and were very good friends at the turn of the 20th Century, and worked together in harmony to produce in effect probably one of the greatest cars and one of the greatest corporate teams the world has ever known, and made the American automobile the envy of the world.

Something dramatic has happened. I do not know what happened, and I hope that these hearings will cast some light on what has gone wrong, but it distresses me that two great companies that together helped to build the American automobile and its safe travel over millions of miles now will not even sit at the same table together at this hearing. Something has to be done.

I would say that another thing that bothers me is that tires were recalled in Saudi Arabia, Malaysia, Thailand, Venezuela, Colombia, and Ecuador before American officials were ever really notified. I mean, the American consumer is not chopped liver, and we ought to know about these things.

However the arrangement between Ford and Firestone was early on in the 20th Century, it is obvious that something has gone wrong now. They keep information from one another, from the U.S. Department of Transportation and worst of all from the American consumer. I am looking for some way to respond to the 47 Georgians who have reported to the National Highway Traffic Safety Administration problems with their tires, some of them while traveling at speeds upwards of 70 miles an hour, and the countless others who are legitimately concerned about their family's safety.

Now, the Ford Explorer has been the highest selling sports utility vehicle among all SUV's. Many of these sales were to families who bought the Explorer based on its being a safer vehicle due to the increased height above other cars on the road. I understand that by the spring of 1999 Firestone had already logged 800 consumer complaints of tread separation, and for over 10 years Ford had been advocating inflating tires to a less than maximum level to decrease chances of roll-over, rather than making structural changes to the automobile.

While the jury is still out on whether the tire and lower psi level combination contributed to some of these accidents, I am disappointed that the Explorer was marketed as a safe family vehicle when problems were actually known.

Now, this corporate behavior is actually unacceptable. What can we do? Well, we can work with the National Highway Traffic Safety Administration to improve their ability to gather information about products sold in the U.S., and increase the resources with which they have to work. I would like to know, Ms. Bailey, about your budgets and whether or not you are able to do the job we expect of you.

I would also like to encourage the National Highway Traffic Safety Administration to continue its work with these companies to ensure that the 6.5 million tires in the voluntary recall are actually changed out.

Last year this committee and the entire Congress passed a law to establish the Federal Motor Carrier Safety Administration. Safety was an integral part of this new agency, and its establishment, and I believe we can aid the National Highway Traffic Safety Administration, an agency which has been focused on safety since its establishment, to better accomplish its goals in promoting highway safety.

I look forward to hearing the testimony of Secretary Slater and Dr. Bailey on their insights and what we can do as a Congress to make sure that no more lives are lost to this tragic situation.

Thank you, Mr. Chairman.

The CHAIRMAN. Thank you.

Senator Snowe.

STATEMENT OF HON. OLYMPIA J. SNOWE, U.S. SENATOR FROM MAINE

Senator SNOWE. Thank you, Mr. Chairman. I want to thank you for holding this hearing, of vital importance to Americans, and you know, listening to a number of the issues that have already been raised in the course of the various hearings last week and now, I find my level of disbelief only increases the more I learn about the indefensible lapse of corporate action and behavior that we are examining here today, and of all the many questions that behavior has raised in my mind, none is more prominent or more illustrative than the issue at hand, the simple question of how is it we even got to this point?

Here we are, at least 88 American lives later, 250 Americans injured, trying to figure out how it is that so many warning signs were seemingly ignored on the way to tragedies that in all likelihood could have been prevented? Numerous red flags have been disregarded over a decade. How is it both companies involved, and Federal regulators, had evidence these tires might be hazardous, Ford Explorers were almost three times as likely to be involved in tire-related fatalities, and as far back as 2 years ago State Farm notified NHTSA about Firestone tire failures, yet no action was taken?

How is it that Ford was concerned enough to take 16-inch Firestone tires off trucks in Venezuela and the Persian Gulf, Malaysia, Colombia, and Ecuador, but apparently not concerned enough to do so here in the United States? When the company issues a recall or obtains evidence concerning a potentially dangerous product being marketed in another country, there should be no question that the American public and U.S. authorities at the very least have a right to know, and they deserve to know.

Now, it is certainly true we cannot change what has happened, but we certainly have an obligation to explore the chain of events that allowed, whether through benign neglect or purposeful withholding of information, or both, these tragedies to occur so that they will not occur again. We owe that much to the families.

I saw a headline in the newspaper the other day that said documents portray tire debacle as a story of lost opportunities. It was a story of lost opportunities to save lives, Mr. Chairman, and that is essentially what this hearing is all about.

And so I say to the corporations who are here today who are implicated in this entire episode, you are not apart from this society. You are a part of this society, and while we can never ensure that every product will be safe at all times under all circumstances, the American public must have some assurance that all actors in bringing consumer products to market, from manufactured goods, to contractors, to the Federal Government, are acting in good faith and in the best interest and the well-being of consumers.

As a Nation and as a society, we believe you should have as broad and as fair a playing field as possible on which you may compete and hopefully succeed. We say if you are willing to assume the risk in the marketplace we are prepared to reward you generously should you build a better mouse trap, a better tire, or a better SUV.

In return, in relative terms, we ask very little. We ask that when we use your products responsibly, that you reveal flaws in your design and manufacturing, that you deal with us honestly. We ask you to assume responsibility for your actions, as we ask each other to do so as individuals, and so we have a right to know, Mr. Chairman, whether or not the companies intentionally withheld information from regulators.

We do have a right to know who knew what when, and what could have been done differently. We have an obligation to ensure and to determine that these tragic circumstances do not repeat themselves ever.

Obviously, we cannot legislate corporate conscience, but we can ensure that the NHTSA budget is adequately funded, and that is where we have an obligation to make sure that we have the kind of funding that ensures oversight and has the regulatory legal framework to ensure that we can protect the well-being of consumers. We owe that much to the American people.

Thank you, Mr. Chairman.

The CHAIRMAN. Senator Dorgan.

STATEMENT OF HON. BYRON L. DORGAN, U.S. SENATOR FROM NORTH DAKOTA

Senator DORGAN. Mr. Chairman, we are glad you are back with us.

We do not live in a perfect world, and mistakes will be made and products will fail. We all understand that. But the story in this circumstance is enormously troubling to me. Both Ford and Firestone in the early cases were sued for tire failures, and those suits were settled with gag orders, and those gag orders prevented the American people and our government safety experts from knowing what the risks were with those products. That is enormously troubling.

I assume some knew what the risks were, but the gag orders prevented most people from knowing what the risks were, and others then purchased products and lost their lives because of that. That is just unforgivable, and I hope that through these hearings and through other mechanisms we discover ways to prevent that from ever happening again, and perhaps through this tragedy of product failure and loss of lives Congress will rediscover merit in the role of Government, in sensible regulations, and in the enforcement of safety standards.

Funding regulatory agencies and giving them the teeth in law to deal with these issues is important. We have been through a couple of decades in which the word regulation was used as a pejorative sort of word around here in Washington, D.C. Sensible regulation in the face of larger and larger corporations that have greater and greater power over the lives of the American people, especially sensible regulations in the area of safety standards, and especially the enforcement of those regulations, ought to be made clear with this case and perhaps in that manner other lives will be saved in the future.

I am anxious to hear from the corporations, and I would say that I would agree with my colleague from Oregon. I think it is important to just step up and admit that these were product failures, significant mistakes were made, the gag orders should not have occurred, the company should have understood this earlier. I mean, let us clear the slate here and start over, but let us also learn from this in a significant way about the merits and value of having sensible regulatory opportunities to enforce safety standards.

The CHAIRMAN. Dr. Frist.

STATEMENT OF HON. BILL FRIST, U.S. SENATOR FROM TENNESSEE

Senator FRIST. Thank you, Mr. Chairman. I will be brief. I do think it is regrettable we are here once again in the U.S. Senate Commerce Committee to discuss how we have failed, and we is in a generic sense, the American consumer.

This recall marks a personal tragedy for many families. A good friend of mine is now dead because he was driving a Ford Explorer with a Firestone ATX tire. Many people have lost loved ones, and industry regulators, Congress has been insufficiently vigilant.

The size and scope of the Firestone recall in question regarding Ford Explorer stability during a blow-out are tremendous, with 90 deaths attributed to this tread separation, and 4.5 million of these tires still on the road today. We must act, we should act, and we should act in an expeditious way.

Three critical goals in my mind: first, we must make the consumer whole. It is imperative that a mechanical failure not be a ticking time bomb that thrusts drivers into deadly accidents. Those tires still on the road must be replaced with greatest urgency.

Second, we must demand accountability, accountability across the board. Finger-pointing between Firestone and Ford and public relations campaigns and even public servants standing on the issue is insufficient, is not right, because they are not the solutions that Americans both demand and, I believe, deserve.

And third, Congress and the executive branch regulators need to enact a more effective warning system, it is crystal clear, in order to shed light, to have full transparency when such defects are there. Lives are at stake. Dr. Gary Haas is dead today. Gary and I operated for years side by side, or in the same operating room at the Massachusetts General Hospital in Boston. Unfortunately in a different situation in a different car with a different tire—as I mentioned, it was a Firestone ATX tire which separated from his Ford Explorer—he would be alive today. He had taken his son to go to college, a great man, a great surgeon who has contributed so much in his life.

There are many personal stories like that, and it is hard to separate from those personal stories, but it is crystal clear that we must and have a responsibility to do all of this. The big statistics, the big numbers are important to use for documentation, but clearly our role is to respond in a reasonable, balanced, intelligent, common sense way, and I look forward to these hearings contributing to that debate and to that discussion and ultimately to the implementation of a policy which will save lives.

The CHAIRMAN. Senator Breaux.

STATEMENT OF HON. JOHN B. BREAUX, U.S. SENATOR FROM LOUISIANA

Senator BREAUX. Welcome back, Mr. Chairman, also, on behalf of all of us.

As millions of Americans, I have a Ford truck and I have Firestone Wilderness tires on it, and that certainly gives me a great deal of concern. I think that what we in this committee need to determine today is what happened, exactly how it happened, where it happened, and even more importantly, what is being done to prevent it from ever occurring again.

I think the confidence that the American public has with people who produce products is in a large extent based on the honesty of those producers of those products. The American people are smart enough to know that products fail. We are not living in a perfect world. But what they do expect from those who do produce products that are determined to be defective is honesty in admitting it and letting the American people know that they are taking the steps immediately to make sure that it does not happen again.

It seems to me that early on there were a lot of bells and whistles and red flags being raised about the safety of these products not just in this country but throughout the entire world, and I think the big problem we have here is the fact that this is clearly a situation that never should have occurred. The product should not have been made defective, of course, but even more importantly than that, we should never have allowed a situation to occur that in effect denied the fact that there was a problem. I think that is as much of a serious problem as the fact that the products were made defective in the first place.

Thank you, Mr. Chairman.

The CHAIRMAN. Senator Gorton.

STATEMENT OF HON. SLADE GORTON, U.S. SENATOR FROM WASHINGTON

Senator GORTON. Thirty, 26, 32, 35, not an audible used, Mr. Chairman, by the Washington Redskins, but answers I have received while inquiring about the proper tire pressure for recalled Firestone tires. Making phone calls over the last few weeks to Ford dealerships, Firestone tire outlets and other tire manufacturers to check on the progress of recall in Washington State, I have gotten conflicting reports from every source about the best tire pressure for Firestone tires on Explorer SUV's.

This is unacceptable even for this relatively short period of time before they are all replaced. It is something that, Mr. Secretary, I would like very much for you to look into promptly, and if you cannot get answers from the companies that are consistent, would you please in your capacity advise people as to how they should be using the tires as long as they are required to continue to use them.

As we work to uncover the truth about where the current system failed, I call upon both Ford and Firestone to do the same thing. Efforts by Ford to shut down production at three assembly plants to make 70,000 new tires available to consumers is a necessary step, one, but only one of which must be taken to remedy a situation that gets worse every day.

After the round of hearings last week, I think it is fair to conclude that all parties in this fiasco are at fault to some degree, but each blames the other. Continued finger-pointing is going to do nothing to ensure the safety of my constituents, or those of any other member of this panel. We must determine the root of the problem in order to ensure that it does not happen again.

The National Highway Traffic Safety Administration cannot allow a situation like this to continue without much more prompt intervention, and it obviously needs the tools in order to do so.

Last week, at one of the earlier hearings, Mr. Chairman, I pointed out that citizens in northern States like my own are very much lagging from the point of view of these replacements. My constituents do not know when they can get their tires replaced. The Firestone Tire Service Center in Seattle says it is a 2- to 6-week wait. The Firestone hotline says that that is highly optimistic. Russ Dean Ford in Pasco, Washington has been waiting for 6 or 7 weeks for any tires, Goodyear, Michelin, Firestone or any other make. They simply do not have them.

The only places in Washington at which you can get prompt replacements are those who manufacture their own tires, and one of those dealerships, Les Schwab, is not requiring the customers to pay for those replacements but is seeking that payment from Firestone itself, which is a highly responsible act.

But Mr. Chairman, we need to know how this took place. We need to know, even more importantly, how we are going to prevent it from taking place again in the future, and we need to be told how people should protect themselves in the time that they cannot get these tires replaced.

The CHAIRMAN. Thank you.

Senator Inouye.

STATEMENT OF HON. DANIEL K. INOUYE, U.S. SENATOR FROM HAWAII

Senator INOUYE. Thank you, Mr. Chairman, and welcome back, sir.

The CHAIRMAN. Thank you, sir.

Senator INOUYE. I believe that all of us should remember that we are not here as prosecutors in a criminal case, nor are we here as lawyers trying a multimillion dollar liability case. We are here to determine whether something went wrong with our regulatory system and, if so, is there something we can do to improve upon that, and so, Mr. Chairman, I am here to listen and learn.

The CHAIRMAN. Thank you, Senator Inouye. I want to thank the witnesses for their patience. The length of the opening statements indicate the deep concern that the members of this committee have.

I would just like to make two comments, Secretary Slater and Ms. Bailey, before we begin. One is that I intend, and I hope that all the members of the committee will join me in writing a letter to the Appropriations Committee asking them to remove the provision which would prohibit the implementation of the consumer rollover rating system study, or system until a study is conducted by the National Academy of Sciences. It is a classic example of inappropriate legislation on appropriations bills, and it also reflects and enhances the cynicism of the American people that special interests can have a provision like that enacted on an appropriations bill.

It was appropriate only to be enacted, if it was necessary, by this committee, the authorizing committee, not the appropriating committees, and I hope all of my colleagues will join me in seeing that that provision be removed by the Transportation Appropriations Committee conferees.

Finally, Secretary, I have discussed with Senator Hollings the importance of acting as quickly as possible. That is why it is important that we hear from you today. Senator Hollings and I believe that it is possible that we could mark up legislation next Wednesday here in the committee that may not be comprehensive legislation, but perhaps we could mark up and report out of the committee and try and get action in the Congress before we go out of session in a very few weeks, and that is why your testimony, Ms. Bailey, is important here today.

Thank you, Secretary Slater.

STATEMENT OF HON. RODNEY E. SLATER, SECRETARY, DEPARTMENT OF TRANSPORTATION, ACCOMPANIED BY DR. SUE BAILEY, ADMINISTRATOR, NATIONAL HIGHWAY TRAFFIC SAFETY ADMINISTRATION (NHTSA)

Secretary SLATER. Thank you, Mr. Chairman. Chairman McCain, Senator Hollings, members of the committee, first of all let me acknowledge how we listened carefully to all of the opening statements, and how very much we appreciate the partnership that we have enjoyed with this committee to work on matters of importance as it relates to transportation and transportation safety over the course of this Administration.

Let me also acknowledge at the outset that I am very pleased, and I know Dr. Bailey is as well, to hear about the specific measures you just mentioned, Mr. Chairman, that will clearly help us in this regard.

I would like to thank you and the members of the committee for holding this hearing, and to begin I want to emphasize yet again the importance of safety to this Administration and to the U.S. Department of Transportation. Safety is our top transportation priority. At the Department of Transportation we have said that it is the North Star by which we are guided and by which we are willing to be judged.

I want to again commend the leadership of the committee and all who have worked with us to really change the focus of transportation and to focus clearly on safety over the course of our work together. Let me also say that I am very pleased to be joined here today by Dr. Bailey, who will come before this committee in but a few days, on Thursday, to seek formal confirmation by the Senate. She has already been recess-appointed by the President, but we appreciate yet again, Mr. Chairman, the opportunity that you and members of the committee afford her to come before you to talk about her commitment to safety and the commitment of NHTSA to safety.

In that regard, as I think about the fact that she will come before you in the next few days, I reflect on the fact that almost 4 years ago I came before this committee and committed to you at that time, as I, too, was seeking confirmation, that I and the 100,000 members of the U.S. Department of Transportation would continue to make safety and security the highest priority of the Department.

I promised to strive to raise our current levels of safety to ever higher heights, and to work with members of this committee, our partners and stakeholders, and the American people in doing so. We have done that, and this committee should be proud of the work that we have done together.

I also appreciate the fact that not only is the record impressive, but we are yet committed to improving on that record. We will do so, as was mentioned by Senator Cleland, as we fully implement the provisions in the Motor Carrier Safety Administration bill that was passed just last year.

We will do so as this committee and the Congress continue to move on pipeline safety legislation, as the Senate unanimously approved this measure just the other day, and the House now takes it up. We will improve the safety of our system as we fully implement the authorizing legislation of TEA–21 dealing with surface transportation and AIR–21 dealing with air transportation matters, both record-level investments not only in safety but also in our transportation system across the board.

Again, the record is impressive. Highway death and injury rates are at the lowest level ever, and commercial aircraft fatality accident rates are again going down, and going even lower as we make commitments to an 80-percent reduction over the next 10 years. Alcohol-related fatalities are at an all-time low; boating fatalities and rail/highway grade crossing fatalities have been reduced as well. Natural gas transmission pipeline failures have been reduced, but will be reduced even more so as we pass the pipeline safety legislation, and serious hazardous material transportation incidents have been reduced as well. Overall, our transportation system is the safest it has ever been.

Having said that, though, and acknowledging the work of NHTSA and others who have worked hard with you to bring those reductions into being, when we consider what Senator Frist said about his dear friend, and we reflect soberly and somberly on the issue that brings us together, we acknowledge that we must do better, and we have to do better in making our system even safer.

All of you have noted that this can be done through a thorough investigation of the recall issues. That is now before us. Also benefiting from the lessons learned as a result of this experience, and then acting proactively, we can provide proactive leadership to provide corrective measures, and to enhance the safety program to ensure that this never, ever happens again.

That is a commitment that we share with you, Mr. Chairman, Senator Hollings, and all of the members of this committee. In addressing you today, then, I want to acknowledge the effort, the serious and forthright effort of NHTSA under the leadership of Administrator Bailey, that they are making to address the investigation and the recall of Firestone ATX and ATX–II and Wilderness AT tires. We also continue to broaden the investigation where necessary, as we did a few weeks ago, with the consumer advisory dealing with another series of tires as it relates to this ongoing investigation.

Dr. Bailey has submitted a statement for the record in which she provides the status of the investigation as it is today. The investigation is continuing, and is continuing on an urgent basis. I have directed the agency to use every means available to conclude the investigation as soon as possible, and to that end I would like to just note for the benefit of the committee that we are reprogramming approximately $1.8 million of our fiscal year 2001 funding to the Firestone investigation from other NHTSA activities, and we will continue to do whatever is necessary.

Mr. Chairman, you mentioned that you wrote me on August 14 to ask that we, quote, review and examine the data collection reporting system used by NHTSA to detect defects, close quote. Today, I would like to note that we have done just that, and then outline a series of legislative actions that I believe we can take. Again, I want to underscore the fact that we are pleased to hear that you and Senator Hollings and other members of the committee have talked and believe that we can move on this matter and do so expeditiously.

Before I do, though, let me urge the members, as you have already acknowledged, to deal with the provision in the appropriations bill as you have expressed. If I may also, Mr. Chairman, I would also like the conferees to be supportive of the .08 BAC provision in the appropriations bill, and also to work with us to remove the provision that would limit us in our efforts to move forward on the hours of service provision so as to correct measures or laws that have been in place for more than 60 years. Clearly, the trucking industry has changed tremendously over that period of time.

But in dealing specifically with the issue at hand, at the top of our list would be a comprehensive bill that we will talk about in greater detail, but that you and I had some communication on back in March of this year, to increase civil penalties for defective noncomplying products, to extend the period within which manufacturers must provide a remedy at no cost to customers, and to require manufacturers to test their products as a basis for their certification of compliance. We hope that it will be possible again to move, as you have noted, this important legislation on an urgent basis. Its provisions will advance the cause of safety.

We would also resubmit our March proposal as part of a larger bill that builds on the lessons, frankly, that we have learned as a result of the Firestone investigation. It is clear that the scope of NHTSA's efforts to obtain data about potential safety defects needs to be broadened, and here before the committee and manufacturers we would like to say that as you make requests for information we, too, would like the companies to present us the same information at the same time.

Again, though, it is clear that the scope of NHTSA's efforts to obtain data about potential safety defects needs to be broadened. To this end, NHTSA needs stronger investigative authority to get the data it needs. Armed with this authority, NHTSA will be in a position to act more quickly in exercising its full authority in dealing with challenges like the one we face.

We would ask the Congress to move expeditiously in providing this new authority, and to give the agency the tools it needs to forge ahead. Our legislative proposal will require manufacturers to report information about potential defects in vehicles or equipment that first come to light, even if that might be in foreign countries if that information relates to, in any way, vehicles or equipment in the United States.

Due to the lack of this requirement, we did not learn about the problems Ford and Firestone were having in Saudi Arabia and other countries until after we opened our own investigation in May of this year. This provision, we believe if enacted will ensure that this kind of situation never happens again.

In the international context, our proposal will seek greater authority to obtain information from foreign governments and organizations concerning possible safety defects that could show up in the United States. We believe that greater interaction with foreign safety agencies will help us get an early warning on problems before they occur, and I would just mention in passing that as we work with our international partners, as we will at an upcoming international transportation safety symposium, on matters dealing with all aspects of transportation, we believe that we can put in place the kinds of relationships that will allow us to really fully implement this kind of authority, once given.

Conversely, we believe that by having this kind of information, we would also be able to provide useful insights to foreign governments if they find themselves in similar situations.

Our new proposal also will seek to close a number of loopholes in our ability to get timely information from manufacturers and other resources about possible defects. We should have full authority to get safety information from manufacturers about their claims experience, as well as warranty and adjustment data.

We need the same type of information from companies that supply original equipment such as brake systems and the like to the vehicle manufacturers, and we need to get timely information about claims information from the insurance industry as well. Our bill will seek authority from all of these parties on each of these measures.

And then I know Senator Bryan also made reference to removing the ceiling on penalties. Our bill will also provide that, Senator, as well.

Finally, Mr. Chairman, we will seek additional funding for NHTSA's safety enforcement program. The Office of Defects Investigation needs to have additional resources both in funding and in people, and we will ask the Congress to provide that amount of resources. We will immediately reprogram, as I have noted, $1.8 million in fiscal year 2001 funding to provide more focus on the Firestone investigation, and we will redirect these funds from other NHTSA programs. We do that because we know it is the right thing to do.

I know that several Members of Congress have either introduced legislation or are considering introducing legislation. We welcome these initiatives, as well as your own, Mr. Chairman, and look forward to working with you and other members of the committee to ensure the enactment of effective legislation that will strengthen highway safety.

I believe that this legislation will give us the expanded authority we need. I pledge that as long as I am Secretary of Transportation we will do everything we can in our power and working with others to use this authority and our existing authority vigorously. My constant message to the employees at the Department of Transportation is that we must be ever visionary and vigilant. We are committed to that end. I can think of no clearer case in which this message must be fulfilled than the one that brings us together here today. We must look to the future to guard against any repetition of the tragedies caused by defective vehicles or equipment.

Mr. Chairman, this concludes my testimony. Dr. Bailey and I would be pleased to respond to any questions you or members of the committee might have.

[The prepared statements of Secretary Slater and Dr. Bailey follow:]

PREPARED STATEMENT OF HON. RODNEY E. SLATER, SECRETARY, U.S. DEPARTMENT OF TRANSPORTATION

Mr. Chairman and Members of the Committee:

Thank you for holding this important full Committee hearing. To begin, I want to emphasize the importance of safety to the Department of Transportation. It is our top transportation priority. It is the North Star by which we are guided and willing to be judged. I want to commend you for your leadership, Mr. Chairman, and that of other Committee members.

Mr. Chairman, almost four years ago when I appeared before this Committee at my confirmation hearing, I pledged to you that I would continue to make safety and security the highest priority of the Department. I promised to strive to raise our current levels of safety to even greater heights. In closing, I want to highlight some of the major accomplishments that this Committee, in particular, was instrumental in helping to achieve. The record is impressive:

- Highway death and injury rates have dropped to all-time lows: from 1.6 to 1.5 deaths per 100 million vehicle miles traveled; and from 133 to 119 injuries per 100 million vehicle miles traveled
- Commercial aircraft fatal accident rate reduced from 0.055 to 0.04 per 100,000 flight hours
- Alcohol-related highway fatalities reduced to 38% from 38.6% as a percentage of the total
- Boating fatalities reduced from 857 per year to 773
- Rail related fatalities per million train-miles reduced from 1.57 to 1.30
- Natural gas transmission pipeline failures reduced from 4,871 per year to 3,754
- Serious hazardous material transportation incidents reduced from 422 per year to 341.

In addressing you today, I want to acknowledge the outstanding effort that NHTSA, under the leadership of Administrator Dr. Sue Bailey, is making to address the investigation and recall of Firestone ATX, ATX II and Wilderness AT tires. Dr. Bailey has submitted a statement for the record, in which she provides the status of the investigation as of today. The investigation is continuing on an urgent basis. I have directed the agency to use every means available to conclude the investigation within six months. Dr. Bailey is available to respond to any questions you may have on the history and progress of the investigation.

Mr. Chairman, you wrote me on August 14 to ask that we "review and examine the data collection reporting system used by NHTSA to detect defects." Today I will outline a series of legislative actions that I believe we need to take. But before doing so, I want to urge members of this Committee, especially those who will serve as conferees on our appropriations bill, to strike language in the bill to effectively block efforts to complete implementation of the consumer rollover rating system proposed by this Department in June.

At the top of our list is the comprehensive bill that we submitted in March of this year to increase civil penalties for defective and noncomplying products, extend the period within which the manufacturers must provide a remedy at no cost to consumers, and require manufacturers to test their products as a basis for their certification of compliance. We hope it will be possible to move this important legislation on an urgent basis. Its provisions will advance the cause of safety.

We will resubmit our March proposal as part of a larger bill that builds on the lessons we have learned in the Firestone investigation.

It is clear that the scope of NHTSA's efforts to obtain data about potential safety defects needs to be broadened. To do this, NHTSA needs stronger investigative authority to get the data it needs. Armed with this authority, NHTSA will move quickly to exercise its authority to the fullest extent possible. I would ask Congress to move quickly to legislate new authority, and give the agency the tools it needs to forge ahead quickly.

Our legislative proposal will require manufacturers to report information about potential defects in vehicles or equipment that first comes to light in foreign countries, if that information relates in any way to vehicles or equipment in the United States. Due to the lack of this requirement, we did not learn of the problems Ford and Firestone were having in Saudi Arabia and other countries until after we had opened our own investigation in May of this year. If this provision is enacted, we can ensure that this will not happen again.

In the international context, our proposal will seek greater authority to seek and obtain information from foreign governments and organizations concerning possible safety defects that could show up in the United States. We will believe that greater interaction with foreign safety agencies will help us get an early warning of problems before they occur here. Conversely, we could provide useful information to foreign governments, if they find themselves in a similar situation.

Our new proposal will also seek to close a number of loopholes in our ability to get timely information from manufacturers and other sources about possible defects. We should have full authority to get safety information from manufacturers about their claims experience, as well as warranty and adjustment data. We need the same type of information from the companies who supply original equipment, such as braking systems, to the vehicle manufacturers. And we need to get timely information about claims information from the insurance industry. Our bill will seek authority for each of these measures. It will also seek to remove the ceiling on penalties for related violations.

Finally, Mr. Chairman, we will seek additional funding for NHTSA's safety enforcement program. The Office of Defect Investigation needs to have additional resources, both in funding and in people, and we will ask the Congress to provide it. We will immediately reprogram $1.8 million of FY 2001 funding to the Firestone investigation from other NHTSA activities.

I know that several members of Congress have either introduced legislation or are considering introducing legislation. We welcome these initiatives, as well as yours, Mr. Chairman, and want to work together to secure the enactment of effective legislation that will strengthen highway safety.

I believe that this legislation will give us the expanded authority that we need. I pledge that as long as I am Secretary, we will do everything in our power to use this authority, and our existing authority, vigorously. My constant message to Departmental staff is that we must be vigilant and visionary. I can think of no clearer case in which this message must be heard: we must look to the future and guard against any repetition of tragedies caused by defective vehicles or equipment.

Mr. Chairman, this concludes my testimony. Dr. Bailey and I will be glad to answer your questions.

PREPARED STATEMENT OF DR. SUE BAILEY, ADMINISTRATOR, NATIONAL HIGHWAY TRAFFIC SAFETY ADMINISTRATION (NHTSA)

Mr. Chairman and Members of the Committee:

I am pleased to appear before you this morning to address the investigation and recall of Firestone ATX, ATX II and Wilderness AT tires. The National Highway Traffic Safety Administration (NHTSA) has learned some valuable lessons from this recall, and now is the time to put those lessons to use in preventing future problems.

Secretary Slater has outlined the legislation that we believe we need. I will discuss what I believe we must do to improve our regulations and our internal procedures. First, let me summarize where we now are in the Firestone investigation.

The Firestone ATX/Wilderness Recall

Firestone originally began producing the tires under investigation in 1991. By the end of 1999, approximately 47 million had been produced. By that time, NHTSA had received 46 reports scattered over 9 years about incidents involving these tires. The tires were on a variety of vehicles, primarily on Ford Explorer sport utility vehicles. In view of the large number of tires that had been produced, the variety of possible causes of tire failure (road hazards, excessive wear, etc.), and the fact that all types of tires can fail in use, the reports that we received did not indicate a problem that would warrant opening a defect investigation regarding these tires. The informal submission by State Farm in 1998 of 21 claims over an eight-year period also did not provide such an indication.

The situation changed rapidly following the airing of a news story by KHOU in Houston on February 7, 2000, that dramatized the question of the tires' safety. In addition to highlighting two fatalities, the KHOU story alluded to a number of other crashes and fatalities.

Upon learning of the KHOU story, we contacted the station to obtain more details about the incidents. They have not given us the information we requested, but the growing publicity generated other reports to us, including several provided by other media outlets and by plaintiffs' attorneys. Over the next few weeks, we were able to verify many of these reports. We opened a Preliminary Evaluation on May 2. At that time, the agency was aware of 90 complaints, including reports of 33 crashes, and 4 fatalities. On May 8 and 10, we sent Ford and Firestone extensive Information Requests asking for information about the tires. At that point NHTSA began a constant communication with both companies, which continues today.

Information accumulated rapidly as a result of the investigation and attendant publicity. By August 1, we had 193 complaints alleging tread separations on these tires, with 21 reported fatalities. In a meeting on August 4, we suggested that Firestone consider recalling the tires. By August 9, when Firestone announced that it was recalling the ATX and ATX II tires, and Wilderness AT tires produced at its Decatur, Illinois, plant, we had over 300 complaints, with 46 reported fatalities. The number has continued to grow. As of August 31 we had 1400 complaints with reports of 88 fatalities and 250 injuries involving the tires covered by the investigation. We will provide information about additional incidents as we collect it.

Firestone has recalled all of the ATX and ATX II tires of the P235/75R15 size manufactured since 1991. It has also recalled Wilderness AT tires of that size made at its Decatur, Illinois, plant, for a total of 14.4 million tires out of the 47 million tires covered by our investigation. As of August 9, Firestone estimated that approximately 6.5 million of the 14.4 million tires included in the recall were still on the road. Ford and Firestone are taking a number of measures to provide replacement tires.

NHTSA is continuing its investigation to ensure that the scope of the recall is proper and that all unsafe tires are recalled. At our request, Firestone and Ford have given us voluminous information about the tires, and we have sent follow up requests for additional information to both companies and to Goodyear Tire and Rubber Company, for a peer comparison. We are continuing to monitor the recall to ensure that all defective tires are replaced promptly.

Our review of data from Firestone has already disclosed that other tire models and sizes of the tires under investigation have rates of tread separation as high or higher than the tires that Firestone is recalling. On August 30, we recommended to Firestone that it expand its recall to include these tires. When Firestone declined to expand the recall, we issued a consumer advisory on September 1 to advise owners of these tires to take actions to assure their safety.

Lessons Learned

As Secretary Slater stated in his opening remarks, we have concluded that we need to get additional legislative authority to enable us to learn of defects that first appear in vehicles or equipment in foreign countries. Such authority could have enabled us to learn of the problems being experienced by Ford and Firestone sooner than we did. If we get the additional authority, I assure you that we will work vigorously to use it.

We have also learned that we can do a better job of using the authority that we already have. In particular, we must accelerate our efforts to bring NHTSA's tire safety standard into line with current practice. We are expanding our review of the standard, which has not been significantly changed since 1968. The vehicles on the road today are much different than those of 30 years ago and are operated at higher speeds now that the national maximum speed limit has ended. We need to amend the standard to address those changes.

A number of claims, and several law suits, had been filed against Ford and Firestone before we became aware of any trend that would indicate a potential defect. We received no information about those events from the companies or from the plaintiffs' attorneys. Our current regulations do not require the manufacturers to give us information about claims or litigation. The existing law gives us broad authority to seek information from vehicle and equipment manufacturers during the course of an investigation. We plan to implement measures that would allow us to track claims and litigation information routinely, even as we are asking Congress to enhance our authority to get this information.

We will also continue our efforts to provide information to consumers about vehicle stability. It seems clear that the failure of these tires presents a greater risk to occupants of sport utility vehicles and compact pickups, with their greater susceptibility to rollover, than to occupants of passenger cars. We are urging the conferees on our appropriations bill for fiscal year 2001 to allow us to complete our implementation of the consumer rollover rating system proposed in June without delay.

Finally, we are taking a hard look at our investigative procedures to make sure we do not miss problems like this in the future. We will ensure that we use our people and resources in the most effective way and seek any additional resources that we may need.

Mr. Chairman, I want to assure you that this investigation is the highest priority in NHTSA. We will remain focused on the investigation, closely monitor the current recall campaign, and seek any expansion of the campaign that may be necessary.

Mr. Chairman, I want to conclude by expressing my thanks to you for holding this hearing. I will be glad to answer any questions you may have.

The CHAIRMAN. Thank you, Mr. Secretary. Thank you for your strong statement.

In a departure from the usual custom of the committee, because of the importance of this issue, two members have arrived who might want to make brief opening comments, Senator Ashcroft and then Senator Rockefeller.

Senator Rockefeller does not. Senator Ashcroft, would you like to make a brief comment?

STATEMENT OF HON. JOHN ASHCROFT, U.S. SENATOR FROM MISSOURI

Senator ASHCROFT. Thank you, Mr. Chairman. I am grateful for this opportunity. I am very concerned, as is everyone on the committee, about how this could have happened. I am saddened, as we all are, by the deaths that bring us to this point. Each of the individuals injured has a name and a face. They had dreams that will not be realized, those that have died, and you do them a great service by calling the meeting together.

I have a unique concern, and that is that the Ford Explorer is made in my home State. In fact, almost half the Ford Explorers that are assembled in the United States are made in Hazelwood, Missouri, and the success of the Explorer has been a source of pride for the workers at the plant and everyone throughout the St. Louis area and, of course, if you are ever in doubt about this, I would be pleased to take you to the plant and we will watch as they drive newly assembled Explorers off the line.

Yesterday, I talked with some of the workers. As you know, the plant has been closed for the past 2 weeks, and will not reopen to assemble the popular Ford Explorer until next Monday, and some have suggested that these workers have it pretty well. 2,000 workers who are not reporting for work are getting paid 95 percent of their income.

Well, I want you to know that they are not content with not working, and they do not see themselves as lucky. They are unsure about their future. Obviously, they do not get overtime, which they normally get, and due to the 15,000 Explorers that will not be produced their profit-sharing is threatened. Nevertheless, I want you to know that these workers did not complain about Ford's decision to close the plant in order to get tires out to consumers as quickly as possible. In fact, I was really inspired by the way the employees had a sense of being proud that the company was willing to take very serious measures to serve the customers.

And since they are not represented here today, I asked these employees to tell me what message they wanted me to give you and, while they could say it much better than I can, I will do my best. They want you to know that what we do here and what we say here makes a difference, and this applies not just to the committee but also to representatives of Ford, Firestone, NHTSA, and the consumer groups, and it makes a difference in their lives.

They do not want careless or reckless allegations about the product that they make. They have valid concerns that allegations that are tossed out even if they do not have data devalues the name of the product that bears not only the Ford name but also the name of the 2,000 workers in Missouri, and they wanted me to share with you the Ford Explorer safety record, which remains substantially above average, and they faxed to my office safety information filed by the United States Department of Transportation, and they asked me to submit this information for the record, and I am pleased to do that.*

The CHAIRMAN. Without objection.

Senator ASHCROFT. Thank you. Just as the rest of the committee, as chairman of the Consumer Affairs Subcommittee I want to know what I can do to make sure this never happens again. I want to thank you for holding this hearing, and I am pleased to be a part of these matters of inquiry.

The CHAIRMAN. Thank you very much. We will have a first round of 4 minutes, and obviously my colleagues would understand, since we have four more witnesses to appear before the committee and it is already 10:30, and so I will begin by thanking you again, Secretary Slater.

Secretary Slater, some questions have arisen about sufficient funding for NHTSA. In the past several years I never heard of any request for additional funding or authorization for additional funding to this committee. Did that happen, to your knowledge?

Secretary SLATER. Mr. Chairman, we have actually provided, in partnership with the committee and the Congress, significant improvements in the NHTSA budget over the years. The President's recommendation this year is higher than either the House or the Senate.

The CHAIRMAN. I was talking about previous years.

Secretary SLATER. In previous years we have also provided an increase in investment, and when we passed TEA–21 again an increase in investment. We did last year because we were trying to use some of what were called RABA funds for the greater investment in safety programs, did not find our efforts successful, but over the years we have done, I think, a good job in giving NHTSA the kinds of resources needed.

Now, clearly, as we deal with matters involving defects and the investigations necessary to fully respond to those, we have found a need to reprogram and to make an additional request in this budget cycle, but I think that working with the committee in past years we have done a good job in providing significant resources to NHTSA for their broad safety purposes, and we have seen significant benefits result from that kind of a commitment.

The CHAIRMAN. At the end of every year around here, we have the President pretty much having his way and billions and billions of dollars are added in the dead of the night, I might add, and I would expect that if there had been any real priority there would have been some of that added.

Joan Claybrook is going to testify, and in her statement she says NHTSA failed to discover this defect because it lacked a proactive program to discover safety defects. She goes on to state, NHTSA was caught flat-footed in this case because it rarely pushes companies to obey the law. The Department allowed GM to resist recall-

* The information referred to was not available at the time this hearing went to press.

ing its 5 million defectively designed 1973 to 1987 pickup trucks with side-saddle gas tanks that exploded in side-impact crashes, and goes on to state several examples in the past.

She goes on to say, NHTSA also has no early warning system in place, and has not been proactive in requiring manufacturer warnings or in using sources of information that are on the pulse-beat of current real world information about vehicle performance.

I do not know if you have seen her testimony or not, but I would like for either you or Ms. Bailey to respond to those allegations by Joan Claybrook.

Secretary SLATER. Well, I would ask Dr. Bailey to join me in responding, but I can tell you that NHTSA has been very aggressive in dealing with matters that pertain to frankly working with the industry and educating the public about important safety measures that could be taken. We have seen significant results from that effort.

I would just give you a few. The use of seat belts, the significant investment of time and resources dealing with educating the public about drunk driving and those sorts of things that have brought about a significant reduction in deaths on our roadways.

We have also over the years made significant improvements in the performance and the safety of automobiles and equipment.

Now, clearly here with the challenge of the Firestone tires and the question involving SUV's and their roll-over tendencies, we have come forward recently with major initiatives to deal with those efforts as well, and with the enhanced program authority that we have made the case for this morning we will be able to bring more focus and attention to these matters, but we have not had a defect to deal with in anyway like this one for more than 20 years.

Now that we have it, we are moving to ensure that measures that were attempted in 1978, when a similar issue arose, that those measures are taken this time, and again I want to commend you, Mr. Chairman and also Senator Hollings, as you have noted your belief that this time we can get the job done, and as an Administration we want to work with you to do just that.

The CHAIRMAN. Ms. Bailey, did you want to respond?

Dr. BAILEY. I think that we may have indicated that much of the information we receive is through consumer complaints. We have a very proactive educational program to try, and increase and, in fact, have increased by thousands per year the number of complaints we get, but it is not enough.

Clearly there was information out there that was not received by NHTSA through that channel. So we are seeking authority to widen our ability to obtain data that could allow us to investigate earlier and be more proactive, specifically the authority you will hear about here, today, not to request, but to require that manufacturers provide us with information from overseas, which in this case could have been instrumental in initiating an investigation sooner, and also here domestically, that we receive information from manufacturers about claims and settlements, which would also have provided us with information that would have instigated a sooner investigation.

The CHAIRMAN. Senator Hollings.

Senator HOLLINGS. Thank you both. Though you say you have not dealt with a defect of this kind, or known of it, in 20 years, and otherwise you did not receive the information, now, there are two reports in the news with respect to one, filing the information that you had, not 20 years ago but more recently, tire defects under Ford, the automobile itself.

And otherwise, there was, if I remember, Beretsky, who said that in 1998 there were only six or seven complaints, in 1999 only eight, whereby now that you are going back and looking, instead of seven there were 76, and instead of eight there were 96 complaints, 47 before the report. Are those reports in the news correct, and what have you done about it?

Secretary SLATER. One of the things about some of the news reports, again they deal with information that we have in some instances requested. They are not yet received. That is why I made the point earlier that one thing we want to do today is to say that as the committee and its team receive information through your investigative efforts, that at the same time the companies provide us with the same information along with, again, following through on the request that we are making.

Senator HOLLINGS. Well, this information is in your files, as I understand it. There have been these complaints there, and misfiled under the automobile instead of tires in the one instance, but otherwise 90-some complaints, where the gentleman is saying we only had eight, in his memo. I mean, what about that.

Secretary SLATER. I agree with that. I want to come back with that, because I think this morning was the first time that we had had notice of some of that, but let me just say that once we started to get the information that was clearly available that we had not gotten earlier, we were able to give a more accurate statement about the degree of the problem.

We were able to raise to 88 the number of deaths, we were able to deal with the 250 or so injuries, but again that was after we got the information we could fully examine and make judgments on. That also led us to making, through our broader investigation, the request for a voluntary recall on some additional series of tires. When that was not done, then we came back with our powers and provided a consumer advisory, so we have responded when we have had the information at our disposal.

Now, again, I would like to ask Dr. Bailey to share with you what she shared with me earlier today about the most recent report we saw this morning, and that you had made reference to.

Dr. BAILEY. I believe you are aware that in Arizona, in 1996, apparently there was information about tread separations and blowouts that was available to Firestone but was not made available to NHTSA. Again, part of our not having been as proactive in the past is, we have not had the regulatory authority to be proactive. We would like to see that changed in the future, and that is part of the work I think we are doing here today.

Specifically, the Secretary is referring to the fact we did not have the information in 1996. But I think it is important to note that after this investigation was begun in May of this year, we did request information from Firestone about any claims, testing, specifically testing as was done in the situation in Arizona. That could have been information that would have been important in terms of this investigation.

I will tell you that we have still not received that information, and we went through that looking for specifically the information about the Arizona testing and have still not received that. So we will be looking into that.

Senator HOLLINGS. Mr. Secretary, just one question. Firestone is a hard learner. They were caught off base 20 years ago, and now here they are in trouble all over again, but I wonder about Bridgestone. The Japanese are known for quality production. Is there a similar National Highway Traffic Safety Administration in Japan, in Tokyo? Do they have a similar agency looking at safety and defects reported? I am wondering about Bridgestone. If I ran Bridgestone I would get rid of Firestone, and I am wondering about Bridgestone itself. Do they have it? What is their record?

I notice one Japanese company that had been keeping secret defects some 20 or 30 years just apologized in the news, but what about Bridgestone? Do you know anything about them at all? Do the Japanese have such a situation or not?

Secretary SLATER. We have safety counterparts in most countries. The agency responsible for vehicle safety in Japan is the Ministry of Transport. I think it is important to note part of the expansion of our authority today would be to allow us to engage internationally with our safety counterparts which are present in most countries, so that we can exchange this type of information.

Senator HOLLINGS. Thank you, Mr. Chairman.

The CHAIRMAN. Thank you. Senator Abraham.

Senator ABRAHAM. Thank you, Mr. Chairman. Let me just follow up on the request, I gather, that will be forthcoming in your legislation with respect to dealing with foreign agencies that work on safety issues. Am I to understand that you are prohibited from interacting with them at this point?

Secretary SLATER. No, we are not necessarily prohibited from interacting with them. Actually, I am in communication with my transportation counterparts all the time. It is just that the enhanced authority would clearly give us the ability to do so in a more constructive way.

Also, when it comes to getting information, how about the performance of certain items internationally? We do not have the authority to require that from manufacturers now, and that is something——

Senator ABRAHAM. That I understand, Mr. Secretary, and I am happy we will be working on that issue, because clearly you do not have access to information from the manufacturers.

The question I guess I am trying to get at is, it seems to me that at least the people who work in NHTSA on safety issues would be monitoring to some extent what is going on in other countries, just as a matter of course, and I guess I have heard today what sounded like an indication that somehow you either are prohibited from doing it or cannot do it and, given the magnitude of some of these recalls, I guess I am wondering why no information, not from the companies here but just from the media or from the international conferences or from other kinds of activities that you might engage in as a part of your job, this information would not have been detected by at least the people who work on safety issues, and I would like to know why that is the case.

Secretary SLATER. Well, I can tell you that most of our international activities across the Department have increased significantly over the last few years, as we have begun to recognize to a greater degree the challenges of a global economy and market, and we are doing a much better job in that arena now than in the past, and that is across the various transportation modes. Dr. Bailey, is there anything specific about NHTSA's work in that regard that might deal more specifically with Senator Abraham's question?

Dr. BAILEY. It is, I would want to characterize it, as more informal, clearly, than it should be. We need clear regulatory cooperation between countries, and that is not the case now, but it is what we are looking for. Obviously, it would be beneficial to exchange this type of essential safety information.

The provision would also authorize the Secretary to reciprocate cooperation received from the regulatory authorities in those other countries, and it would require that special measures be taken, because you can imagine for trade this is a real issue, to protect any confidential commercial information and nonpublic predecisional materials be disclosed to or received from a foreign Government in furtherance of regulatory cooperation, and it is modeled on the Food & Drug Administration, 21 C.F.R.

Senator ABRAHAM. Thank you. I think my assumption is the committee is going to be very receptive to try and formalize the ability to collect information or to exchange it.

I chair a subcommittee of the Judiciary Committee on Immigration, and while we do not have any, to my knowledge, formal responsibility or authority to find out what is happening with respect to immigration policies in other countries, I only have two people on that staff, but they keep pretty close tabs on what is happening in other countries, and I guess it is a little bit of a surprise that none of this information was known to anybody at NHTSA, in light of the magnitude of it.

Let me just ask another question. In the House hearings last week it was revealed that a claims researcher for State Farm Insurance Company contacted NHTSA on three separate occasions between July 1998 and December 1999 to discuss concerns about these tires and the related accidents, and my first impression when I heard about it was, this is some sort of call that maybe was made out of the blue to a hotline, or something like that.

But the State Farm witness' testimony indicated the following. They said most of the data that was provided to NHTSA was—this is an exact quote—was in response to a request from the agency. On occasion, however, we advised NHTSA of potential claims trends being reported from our field offices.

The decision to initiate a contact with NHTSA is based on a number of factors, including whether research of our information reveals a number of similar reports or cases with possible safety implications, a particular vehicle model within a specific period of time.

We are in regular communication with NHTSA by e-mail and telephone on a wide range of related issues. In a year we share information on approximately 150 investigations.

So it seems that the actual fact is that State Farm works regularly with you in terms of this kind of information exchange, examining crash data and supplying you periodically at least with information and tips about potential problems, so I am just wondering what your response is to the fact that this information was provided on three separate occasions. How do you explain the lack of followup? Is there a particular reason that no additional action was taken at the time of these reports, or did they not rise to a certain level of relevance? How do you do that, and what should we know about that as we proceed legislatively?

Dr. BAILEY. First, the important part of the question is that in fact those 21 claims were over 6 years, so we were getting several claims per year, while they were getting hundreds, or we were getting hundreds of complaints about other tires. And so put into perspective those 21 would still not have instigated the investigation at that time.

Now, let me also say it was part of an informal arrangement, or a relationship with State Farm. It is the only relationship we have with an insurance company. I would like to see us in the future formalize relationships with not only State Farm but others, so it does not come in in the way it did this time, which, by the way, was unsolicited, and by e-mail. And there is only one contact that is recalled at this time, and this was 2 years ago, and we were receiving hundreds of those sometimes in a week.

I have personally seen the e-mail. The e-mail said, quote-unquote, we have "noticed" these claims. I went over the material, and we have since gone over that material. It would not have instigated, as I say, an investigation at that time, given the number over the years, when 40 million tires had been produced.

Senator ABRAHAM. The only followup I just want to finish with is this. My impression is that what triggered NHTSA's greatest scrutiny most recently was the reports of a Houston television station investigation. Was that a key element in your decisions here to now press forward?

Dr. BAILEY. It was a key element, because if you remember, much of our work is done based on the complaints we get from consumers. Those complaints doubled after that KHOU hearing, and that was what created in March the impetus for us immediately to start an initial assessment and then begin the investigation in May, which I believe prompted the recall in August.

Senator ABRAHAM. I would only say, obviously, we will want to follow up with written questions, but I am a little bit concerned that people who do this professionally in terms of claim adjustments at State Farm and work with you on a semiformal basis did not get the kind of attention that a TV report did, and I guess that troubles me to some extent, but we look forward to finding out more from you as we proceed through the process.

I have gone over my time. I apologize, Mr. Chairman.

The CHAIRMAN. Senator Bryan.

Senator BRYAN. Thank you very much, Mr. Chairman.

I have several questions, and I realize that we are on a short time constraint so, if possible, if I can get a yes or no answer to my question, I would be appreciative.

We are told that, adjusted for inflation, that NHTSA's budget today with respect to enforcement is about half of what it was two decades ago, and that only 20 investigators are in the field that are engineers that are looking into vehicle safety defects. My first question, is that true, and if so, what are your budget recommendations for us in light of our experience with Firestone and Ford?

Secretary SLATER. Well, the answer is, for the most part true. We have again seen increases over the past 3 or 4 years, and that has been good, but we do need to have additional resources here, and the President's budget, our proposal, would provide significantly more resources.

Senator BRYAN. And you are satisfied, Mr. Secretary, the President's budget request is enough to do the job?

Secretary SLATER. We are. Now, we also are going to submit for consideration a request for an additional $9 million that would be used primarily to help us deal with the current challenge of the Firestone recall. We have already reallocated $1.8 million to expedite that process, and we are going to make a request for an additional $9 million.

Senator BRYAN. I thank you for the brevity of your response. You are indicating the President's budget request plus $9 million is what you are asking?

Secretary SLATER. No. The $9 million would be included, but what we do is, we actually reprioritize some of the resources for this particular purpose.

Senator BRYAN. I think I understand. So you are saying you think that the President's budget request, with this reprioritizing, is adequate to do the job?

Secretary SLATER. Yes.

Senator BRYAN. I do not believe I heard an answer to the distinguished Ranking Member's question about the data base. What we are led to believe is that the agency failed to detect early on some of these complaints because there is a different data base for tires and a different data base for automobiles. Can you tell me, is that true, and if it is, what are you doing to merge those data bases so we do not have a similar problem?

Dr. BAILEY. I think it is important to note, again, to keep this in perspective, that even with the State Farm data which was filed, by the way, and which I have at my disposal, and with the 46 complaints we received over almost a decade, out of 47 million tires, even combined that would not have instigated an earlier investigation.

Senator BRYAN. Are you saying, Dr. Bailey, that even if the merged data base, if the data base had been merged or combined, that still would not have been enough to trigger——

Dr. BAILEY. Correct, because that would have been probably less than 10 a year, while we were getting hundreds of complaints about other tires, so it probably would have not caused the investigation.

What would have caused the investigation was to have information from overseas, and all of that claims data that was out there, and that is what we are seeking here today, and what can remedy this.

Let me just answer your question about the information system, because you are right, we have, as is often the case, in corporations, and around the world, as we have come into a computerized era, that we have stovepipes of systems. We need the additional funding to coordinate and integrate those systems so that we can bring all that data together that we are seeking here today for the future.

Senator BRYAN. And Dr. Bailey, does the President's budget provide sufficient money for you to merge the data bases, or consolidate them in some way, that it provides an earlier trip warning system? I take it for the record the answer is yes.

Dr. BAILEY. The answer is yes.

Senator BRYAN. I thank you.

Now let me go over some of the recommendations that have been made. One of the criticisms is that the tire safety standard itself is 32 years old, at a time when many tires in America were bias ply, not radials. Radials last longer than bias ply, and it has been suggested that the safety standard needs to be changed with respect to radial tires.

My question is, 1) do you agree it needs to be changed, and 2) where are we in that process?

Dr. BAILEY. It is an old standard. It needs to be changed. We are in the process. We are in fact looking to the manufacturers to give us their input on that. In October, next month, we are moving ahead with that, and clearly need to update those standards.

Senator BRYAN. So that process is moving forward, and you will have a sufficient budget to move forward in that process, is that correct?

Dr. BAILEY. Yes, sir, with the additions.

Senator BRYAN. Finally, your comments with respect to the suggestion we ought to increase civil penalties. We ought to increase the statute of limitations, require record retention for longer periods of time—there is a whole series of these you are familiar with. Do you agree with those and, if so, are they going to be included in the letter you will be sending to our chairman, who I will be looking forward to working with and supporting bipartisan legislation?

Secretary SLATER. That is correct, Senator. You should know that those recommendations and components of the bill were actually put together through leadership and advice on the part of NHTSA.

Senator BRYAN. And is it possible for each of us as members of the committee to have access to that letter?

Secretary SLATER. Yes.

Senator BRYAN. We do look forward to working with the chairman.

Mr. Chairman, my time has expired. I thank our panel for their responses, and again thank you for your leadership.

The CHAIRMAN. Thank you, Senator Bryan.

Senator Burns.

Senator BURNS. Mr. Chairman, I have questions for the next panel. I have no questions for this one. I have a previous engagement I have got to make at 11 o'clock, so I pass on this one. Thank you very much.

The CHAIRMAN. Thank you. Senator Wyden.

Senator WYDEN. Thank you, Mr. Chairman.

Thank you, and Ms. Bailey, as you heard me say earlier, my big concern is that there may not be another committee sitting here in 20 years going over essentially the same issues which are not very different than the Congress looked at 20 years before, so to that end it seems to me we have got to come up with the right mix of preventive and enforcement policies, and I have a question in each area.

On the preventive side, which ought to be the centerpiece of any strategy, you all have adopted this approach where mechanics for the Federal Aviation Administration reports safety problems that they encounter while servicing aircraft. What would you think of a similar approach for automobile service requirements, tire service centers, or independent mechanics, so that we could even get a jump start on a kind of early warning system, rather than waiting for your investigators to try to bring it forward? Would you all support that kind of approach? Mr. Secretary?

Secretary SLATER. Yes. Yes, and clearly here, Senator, just in a general sense I think there are lessons to be learned as we look across the transportation spectrum where we can actually employ things that have been tested, procedures that have been tested in other modes, and I think this is a fine example of one.

I would say this, though, and hopefully there may be other questions on this particular matter, but in order to do that it is very important that we deal with this issue mindful of not overly criminalizing certain actions, because in order to get that kind of input by people at the grassroots level, the ground level, they really have to feel free to share information with you, and we have done that across the aviation spectrum I think quite well, and it would be very important for that same kind of message to be a part of this sort of approach in this area.

Senator WYDEN. I intend to work with the Chairman and Senator Hollings on that, because it seems to me what has worked in the FAA area could work in this area as well. That would be the first line of a kind of preventive strategy, but your response to me touches on the second area that I want to go to, and that is that if there is an egregious violation, one where a company knowingly is aware that their product is going to cause death, or serious injury, is it reasonable to say that in those instances a criminal penalty should apply?

Now, 20 years ago John Moss, somebody who was a real hero of mine, said that that should have been done. We are not here as prosecutors, as the distinguished Senator from Hawaii said earlier. My question to you is, starting with a preventive kind of strategy which I think ought to be the focus of our work, and I think you are absolutely right about doing that carefully so as to encourage people to come forward, should we say in addition to that, for truly flagrant violations, where a company knows that the product is going to kill or maim, is it appropriate to have a criminal penalty, or a criminal statute that would allow for criminal penalty in that instance?

Secretary SLATER. Senator, the short answer there is clearly yes.

Now, after saying that, though, I would hasten to say our approach has been to provide generally three means for responding once your investigation reveals certain information. One would be through an administrative civil penalty, and to do that only after a full-fledged evidentiary hearing, probably involving an administrative law judge. Also, a judicially enforced civil penalty, which the NHTSA statute already provides, and we would increase the levels of those penalties as has been noted, at one point we were talking about up to, like, about $4 million, but we are talking now about just eliminating the ceiling so that you could deal with whatever the situation would warrant.

But then beyond that, you know, as you have noted and as you have stated, for egregious circumstances criminal penalties would be appropriate, where it can be demonstrated beyond a reasonable doubt that a person subject to the NHTSA motor carrier safety requirements intentionally violated them with serious consequences.

Senator WYDEN. I want to explore that with you, and I want to explore that with the Chairman and Senator Hollings. Something like this needs to be approached with great care, and I want to make it clear that I believe that the centerpiece of our strategy ought to be a preventive kind of approach, but I also think that if we are talking about companies who have knowledge of a pattern of activity that can kill and maim, that must be treated with the strongest possible deterrent, which would involve a criminal penalty, and I look forward to the bipartisan approach the Chairman is going to be taking, and I yield.

The CHAIRMAN. Dr. Frist.

Senator FRIST. Thank you, Mr. Chairman. As I listen to the testimony and the discussion and the questions, it seems clear to me that NHTSA's biggest challenge, or problem, or deficiency, something that must be addressed, is a lack of an ability, and it may be in part resources, and it may be direction and leadership, but an ability to coordinate the various data bases, the various information which does exist.

It is clear that Firestone certainly had significant warranty claims information. Ford seemed to be aware of an increased propensity for the Explorer to roll if those tires were fully inflated. We talked about State Farm in their contact with NHTSA with safety trend information that never quite made it, and according to news reports yesterday it would have appear the plaintiffs bar feared sounding the alarm at NHTSA would give defendants advance opportunity to defend themselves, lack of access to information from overseas.

With all of that as background, what will you be doing to ensure better communication, addressing the communication of this lifesaving information?

Dr. BAILEY. I think that is the essential work here today, to increase our authority to obtain information from anywhere in the public domain. In a global marketplace we need information from markets outside the United States and we were not receiving that. I think what we have missed here is the bulk of the material that was not our authority to receive. So we are asking this committee to work with us so that we can obtain the authority that would have given us the opportunity to protect Americans and save lives.

Senator FRIST. Beyond the authority, and Senator Bryan began in his questioning talking about standards outside of information, which obviously we are going to move on aggressively to address the authority issue internally, we mentioned the updating standards. Could you give us several other examples of things you are doing immediately internally that do not require legislation to improve the communication?

Dr. BAILEY. Immediately we have reassigned the staffing patterns so we can deal with this investigation, and realigned our resources as well. But all of that is ongoing now, and you are hearing that we are also going to be reprogramming $1.8 million so that this investigation will be expedited.

The Secretary has been behind us 100 percent in moving this faster than any investigation we have ever done before. But I think the bigger question here, and what I hear you asking, is what can we do so that we are able to be as highly efficient as this regulatory body should be in the future. And one of the main ones you are hearing is to have a data base that will let us make use of this new information we will have the authority to obtain, but also to make use of information that we have previously had authority to obtain but was in a form that did not necessarily provide information that gave us the full picture. It would not change the course of events, our internal issues surrounding information systems in this investigation. It is the bigger picture that is the issue for the Firestone question.

Senator FRIST. One just final followup to that from earlier is when you said the 46 reports and 45 reports would not have met, or the implication would not have met the threshold to throw up a red flag, to me that suggests the triggers are going to be quantitative and not qualitative. Are you confident that in the sophistication of a data base that you will have appropriate flags that go beyond just the quantitative that might not meet the denominator, or the ratio that would, through some algorithm would kick it out?

Dr. BAILEY. As one scientist to another, let me say that we do tend to think in terms of statistics and numbers and percentages and formulas, and my staff has been, I think, struggling with the fact that I have imposed that on them in this last couple of weeks. At the same time, they have always had in place threshold guidelines, which are good guidelines, and we are going to continue to apply, which of course make use of the data we are talking about here today, and those specific numbers. But they also look at other situations, such as catastrophic crashes and fatalities, and factor those variables in as well, and we will continue to do so.

Senator FRIST. Thank you. Thank you, Mr. Chairman.

The CHAIRMAN. Thank you.

Senator Inouye.

Secretary SLATER. Mr. Chairman, I think we should also mention that we are going to use some of the additional resources to promote our hotline and its use, and also use our web site to provide better communication means with the broader public, and so we are definitely going to use the power of technology, along with our relationships with manufacturers, with insurance companies and others to get more data, and then streamline the process for sharing that data across not only the various offices within NHTSA but also to a greater degree across the Department as a whole. Dr. Bailey and NHTSA are taking a leadership role in that regard, and the additional resources and authority will help them in that regard.

The CHAIRMAN. Senator Inouye.

Senator INOUYE. Thank you.

Dr. Bailey, you have indicated that you initiated a preliminary evaluation on the Firestone case in February of this year, and this was prompted by a Houston, Texas TV program.

Dr. BAILEY. The preliminary evaluation was May 2, but yes, the KHOU was February, and that did prompt the initial assessment.

Senator INOUYE. And you have indicated that had you been aware of some of the problems in overseas posts you would have acted earlier.

Dr. BAILEY. Yes, sir.

Senator INOUYE. Mr. Secretary, you have also indicated that had you had better information from abroad you would have acted earlier.

Secretary SLATER. That information, coupled with what we have, would have given us more information on which to base a decision, and we would have acted earlier, yes.

Senator INOUYE. I have been here for a few years, and during these few years administration after administration has tried to impress upon me how effective our embassies are. Each embassy has two very senior members, a professional defense attache and a commercial attache, and we are very proud of them. They feed us information of all sorts. We have better information on the weather in the Soviet Union than we have here, for example.

When did you first learn about the Malaysian situation?

Secretary SLATER. It was only after we began our own investigation.

Senator INOUYE. The commercial attache did not tell you that Firestone and Ford got involved in some sort of activity there in 1998?

Secretary SLATER. We did not have that kind of information before we began our own investigation.

Senator INOUYE. Did the commercial attache advise your agency that in 1999 Ford had recalled 6,800 vehicles to replace the Firestone tires? That is big news, is it not?

Secretary SLATER. Well, it should be, but again we just did not have the information.

Senator INOUYE. The State Department did not pick up the phone and tell you that we have got problems in Saudi Arabia? What about Venezuela? Did the embassy there communicate with you, or the State Department?

Secretary SLATER. No. We found out about the recalls afterwards.

Senator INOUYE. This is supposed to be the age of information technology, and we are not getting this. Where is the e-mail, and you have got a letter and all of that business.

Secretary SLATER. I think, Senator, actually what we are now doing as a Department, is reaching out to our counterparts across the globe and really strengthening our own communications, where we recognize that transportation does not end at the border's edge, but that it is now international in its reach, it is the tie that binds. We have clearly moved from a period where an interstate tied cities and communities of our Nation together to a point now where the waterways and the airways, and in some instances in the hemisphere railroads are tying this country together with other countries in the world, and we have to be more concerned than we have been in the past about how that is impacting all of our countries, and how we have to share information.

Quite frankly, we have not been as focused on this kind of issue as we are now. We as a Department have recently held internationally the Asian meetings with all of our counterparts in Chicago just at the end of last year, with Africa. We have traveled much more extensively.

I just think more recently we have given more focus to this kind of issue and these kinds of challenges, and that is why we have made specific provision in a more comprehensive bill that deals with how it can better enhance the communication flows with our counterparts around the world, and that is what we are trying to achieve here, something that has never been a matter of utmost consideration, but it is now.

Senator INOUYE. Mr. Chairman, I would like to receive some word from the State Department as to whether they knew about these problems.

The CHAIRMAN. I think Senator Hollings and I would like to join you in a formal inquiry on that issue.

Senator HOLLINGS. And the Commerce Department. You know, we had the agricultural attache reporting directly to the Secretary of Agriculture. We changed in the early 1980's a law whereby the commercial attache reports to the Secretary of Commerce, so we will ask the Secretary of Commerce.

The CHAIRMAN. Senator Snowe.

Senator SNOWE. Thank you, Mr. Chairman. Thank you, Secretary Slater and Ms. Bailey, for being here this morning.

A few questions. Ms. Bailey, as I understand, State Farm Insurance had 70 reports of various claims with respect to these accidents, is that correct?

Dr. BAILEY. What was the number?

Senator SNOWE. 70 total.

Dr. BAILEY. You would have to tell me over what period.

Senator SNOWE. From 1998, 1999 the request that you made in April of 2000.

Dr. BAILEY. Yes, over those years it did increase.

Senator SNOWE. Were there about 70 in all between 1998 and 1999? How many are we talking about?

Dr. BAILEY. I will get you the number. The number, I know, prior to the year 2000 that we knew about from State Farm was 21, but I will get the additional number.

Senator SNOWE. But in response, in Joan Claybrook's testimony it says on April 25, 2000, in response to a NHTSA request, 70 reports covering 1996 through 2000 were sent. Would that be correct?

Dr. BAILEY. I know there were additional reports.

Senator SNOWE. So there could be about 70. Now, in that 70 or so, were there deaths, fatalities related to those claims?

Dr. BAILEY. In that group above the 21 I believe there were, but again I would need to get the number for you.

Senator SNOWE. I gather you make the decision, the agency makes the decision with respect to what is statistically significant, is that correct?

Dr. BAILEY. Correct.

Senator SNOWE. So why would not fatalities raise a red flag with respect to these claims?

Dr. BAILEY. A fatality itself would not necessarily, as tragic as that is it would not necessarily alone instigate an investigation.

Senator SNOWE. It would not?

Dr. BAILEY. One fatality would not. Let me say that there is a difference between some equipment on vehicles that would, that one fatality or one failure would instigate, or just a few complaints would instigate, an investigation when it is a piece of equipment that should never fail, like a safety seat for a child, or a seat belt. But tires do fail on a regular basis, and so that has to be accounted for.

Senator SNOWE. How many fatalities would be involved, ordinarily, with tire failures that would come to your attention, especially by an insurance company that dealt with numerous claims and was talking about a pattern of problems, not just one or two isolated incidents?

Dr. BAILEY. Keep in mind I believe in that second group that there in fact still would be very few fatalities, and those words just do not even seem to go together.

I do not mean to in any way reduce our concern, or invalidate the tragedy that has occurred here. But let me just tell you that of 46 complaints we did have there was one fatality in that 46 in the decade preceding. But of all the tire failures that we were aware of, that was a small number and still did not instigate an investigation, so it is not the fatality, it is the nature of what it is we are investigating and the rest of the numbers.

Senator SNOWE. But would it not be unusual that State Farm would contact NHTSA and say there is a problem here?

I do not know. I am asking you. Would you say that is unusual? We are talking about a pattern of problems. Would you find that unusual that the insurance company would bring that to NHTSA's attention?

Dr. BAILEY. No, because we had a relationship where we communicated and provided information to State Farm, and they to us.

Senator SNOWE. Have you decided that it is a tire problem, or a Ford Explorer problem, or both?

Dr. BAILEY. At this time I think we are dealing with a tire problem, but as part of our investigation we will also explore the possibility of a combination.

Senator SNOWE. Now, just looking at this *New York Times* article the other day, it had a chart that said red flag. Again, based on Federal data, that showed that fatal accidents involving Ford Explorers were nearly three times as likely to be tire-related compared to fatalities involving other sport utility vehicles or cars. That data also shows the number of accidents involving Explorers compared with other SUV's in the late 1990's. You can see this chart. Did that ever come to your attention in any way? The way the data comes to the agency, would they be aware of this kind of a chart, using their own information?

Dr. BAILEY. Indeed, we are well aware of that, and again it is part of the ongoing investigation, because we are concerned about the roll-over capability. And in fact, as you have heard the Secretary testify today, that is why we are looking to having a roll-over rating system, and hope that the restriction on us to begin that work will be removed.

Senator SNOWE. So it could be a combination problem. You have not made that determination yet. You are looking at it?

Dr. BAILEY. Correct.

Senator SNOWE. Have you decided——

The CHAIRMAN. Senator Snowe, your time is up.

Senator SNOWE. Thank you, Mr. Chairman.

The CHAIRMAN. I apologize. Senator Ashcroft.

Senator ASHCROFT. Thank you, Mr. Chairman. I want to try and clarify a couple of things that I am not sure whether I understand them. Is it your view that you do not have the authority to receive certain information now, or that you do not have the authority to compel certain information be collected?

Dr. BAILEY. We do not have the authority to require a manufacturer to provide. If we request the information, yes, it can be provided.

Senator ASHCROFT. So what you need is the authority to compel information. That is what you will be asking for, and not to receive information, because you have already got the ability to get the information.

Dr. BAILEY. To obligate the manufacturer to provide that, yes, sir.

Senator ASHCROFT. It occurs to me that in air traffic we get very sensitive about analyzing fatalities and wrecks, and I just wondered in automobile accidents the people who investigate those accidents, who are they, and it seems to me they are fragmented. They are not organized, and it might be that getting that information, is it the insurance companies who have the broadest reach in that respect, or are there law enforcement agencies that have a broad reach there? Could you enlighten me on that?

Secretary SLATER. It is a combination of both.

Senator ASHCROFT. You have city police departments, local sheriffs, highway patrols, then some Federal law enforcement authority, and to what extent do they ascertain or try to identify causes for these accidents, and do they report to you on them?

Dr. BAILEY. One of the most sophisticated fatality reporting systems is our FARS data, and that comes from throughout the Nation, State by State and down to the local level of law enforcement.

As the Secretary says, we get information from all sources, and again I would want the consumers to know that we are looking for direct information from them. That is our number 1 way of obtaining the data. But we also do have this FARS data, which is from law enforcement. But as you hear here today, we did not have access to the bulk of the information that could have made a real difference here, which was that claims data.

Senator ASHCROFT. Doctor, I think you suggested that you have certain statistical guidelines. When you get information about failures in systems, is that information related to the consequence of the failure? In other words, does the failure associated with the fatality have a different weight in triggering investigation, and I think this is kind of following up on what Senator Snowe has said.

I could see a high number of incidents that did not relate with any sort of real threatening or life-threatening problem, but if you get—it seems to me the threshold should be lower if those problems are associated with fatalities or serious injuries. Is that the way you are set up?

Dr. BAILEY. Yes, sir, it is, and that is why we compile the FARS data. But this is one more piece to those, to the puzzle here of the way in which we use that information system.

I should say, by the way, that NHTSA itself also conducts about 5,000 crash investigations a year.

Senator ASHCROFT. I see my time is almost up, but you want to have additional information from overseas. Is there any set of protocols which would entitle you to that information, or would you just try to get it by virtue of cooperation with other nations?

For instance, are there nations party to international agreements that require or provide for exchange that we are not a party to now? Is there a need for, in your judgment, some sort of international protocol for this sharing? I can understand why you would like to have the information. Is there a mechanism for delivering the information, assembling it that exists that we are not participating in, or is there a need for that to be developed?

Dr. BAILEY. There is a need for that to be developed.

Senator ASHCROFT. So mere authority to get the information would not automatically mean we have got it right now. You really think there needs to be some sort of routine developed whereby the information is shared.

Dr. BAILEY. There are two issues here. One is the exchange of information between our safety counterparts in other countries, and more specifically, in this case with Firestone, the information that relates to what was known by a manufacturer about a possible defect that was information contained in a subsidiary in another country. That is the ability to obtain information we are requesting.

Secretary SLATER. We want the manufacturers to be required to give us that information just as they are required to give us that kind of information when they are dealing with situations here in the U.S. We want that same information when they have got a situation in some other country that might be in some way connected with a product that is in use here in the U.S., and that is what we do not have as a requirement in this instance.

Also, Mr. Chairman, if I may just briefly, we are working with our foreign counterparts on a number of harmonization efforts, and some of those deal with equipment, but this is something that is very new when it comes to the work that we do with our international counterparts, and it is work that is increasing, and so we just want more of an ability and authority and guidance when it comes to engaging in that kind of effort with our international partners.

The CHAIRMAN. I thank you both. I appreciate your patience, and appreciate your answers. We have a lot of work to do between now and next Wednesday. I look forward to working with you. Thank you for appearing.

Senator Rockefeller, my profound apologies.

Senator ROCKEFELLER. Mr. Chairman, it is not your fault. I just slipped in through the back door.

The CHAIRMAN. If you would remain until Senator Rockefeller has completed his comments.

Senator ROCKEFELLER. I just want to make an observation which I think is ironic and interesting. For the last—and that is the difference between the Department of Transportation—Chairman McCain I think has done a very correct thing in having us all sign this letter asking for something which was taken out of appropriations, put back in both last year and this year, but then I compare what you do in the FAA for the certification of an airplane, of a new airplane, and this, and it is a stunning difference.

Many, many more people use vehicles than use airplanes. I do not know the exact figures, but it has got to be a huge difference, and I am not trying to say we should do one for the other, because you know, it is Ford, Chevy and Chrysler and others that develop their cars, and then unfortunately it is often when we come to examples of this sort that you all come in on the contrary with the FAA Schools and Libraries Corporation.

I have been involved with a new corporate jet called the SJ30–2 for 8 years, and it has, I think, about 72,000 parts, parts—I mean, little parts, huge parts. Even precertification, even before what they call the roll-out can take place, FAA has inspected every single one. DOT, in other words, has inspected every single one of those parts.

Then they go on to the extremely complex business of the testing of the in-flight capability of the airplane, and it is a stunning amount of information. Everything about that information is known by DOT, everything. There is not one single thing, not one single part which has not been thoroughly analyzed, tested, inspected, and it is a multiyear process.

It is very frustrating but very safe, and I just want to make the point, Mr. Chairman, that it is just an interesting sort of a difference within DOT, that on the one hand, you cannot precertify Ford Explorers or anything else, but you do complain of a lack of regulatory authority, a little bit like the Surface Transportation Board complains of a lack of regulatory authority. We routinely do not do anything about it, and I think under Chairman McCain we are about to do something about that, and I am not suggesting regulatory authority ought to govern all of this, but it is a stunning difference between a mode of transportation that carries fewer people, as opposed to a mode of transportation that carries far more people.

You are all over one, and limited to about 20 engineers out in the field, and then you have to wait until something happens, and I just want to make that observation.

Thank you, Mr. Chairman.

The CHAIRMAN. Please respond, Secretary Slater. I think it is a very interesting point.

Secretary SLATER. It is, and with the question that Senator Ashcroft was asking a few minutes ago, I thought about the comparison that was being made, but wanted to be more direct in response to him.

You should know that we have worked very hard as a Department, and especially NHTSA, to make the point that it should be unacceptable that we sort of accept as a matter of course the loss of 40,000 people on our roadways on an annual basis. We have worked very hard to bring that number down, at one point over 40 percent, 41 percent of all of the automobile crashes involved alcohol. Fortunately, through our efforts, working with MADD and other organizations, we are down below 40 now at about 38 percent, and continuing to drive that number down.

.08 would be a measure that would help us in that regard. We have also worked with the Congress to do things like bring into law the zero tolerance for youth when it comes to alcohol and driving some years ago during the Reagan Administration with the leadership of the Congress. And at the time we were able to pass the 21 age for drinking for youth.

And so we have I think started to do things to demonstrate that it is not acceptable to have those kinds of numbers. And we have worked in partnership with the automotive industry to make those improvements as well.

Just one example and I will close. With our partnership with New Generation Vehicles, we are not only trying to get greater efficiency as it relates to gasoline mileage, about 80 miles per gallon, but we are also testing to ensure that there is no safety compromise, that there is the performance and ultimately that it will be something that is affordable so all of the American people can enjoy.

But I think that NHTSA focusing on prevention is really starting to make some significant headway on this issue. And it is not where it is with aviation. We have got 52,000 of our 100,000 employees who are in aviation. We are now trying to get a few more in NHTSA and some additional authority. And I think we are moving in a common sense approach and way to addressing these issues in ways that are more common than different. And I appreciate you and others who have raised the issue over the course of the hearing.

The CHAIRMAN. Thank you. And again, my apologies, Senator Rockefeller. Senator Hollings has a followup.

Senator HOLLINGS. Mr. Secretary, the records show that NHTSA's had 99 million recalls in the last 5 years. I take it all of those have been voluntary. Can you correct me? How many have you ordered in the last 5 years?

Dr. BAILEY. You are correct, sir. The vast majority are voluntary.

Senator HOLLINGS. Have you ordered any recalls in the last 5 years that you know of?

Dr. BAILEY. Twenty percent overall, not in the last 5 years. Twenty percent are mandatory. But again, it is the real minority. We are really——

Secretary SLATER. That is NHTSA influenced. And you could argue in this instance——

The CHAIRMAN. Let us answer Senator Holling's question. In the last 5 years, how many recalls? What percent?

Secretary SLATER. I do not know that we have it for the last 5 years, Mr. Chairman. We will see.

Senator HOLLINGS. Well, we have it. They just gave it to me.

Secretary SLATER. That is why we said in the beginning we would like to have the information you have.

Dr. BAILEY. The answer is over 60 percent of the vehicles recalled are a direct result of our investigations. But the answer to the last 5 years, none.

Senator HOLLINGS. That is what I was saying. All of them (information) have been voluntary. Thank you, Mr. Chairman.

The CHAIRMAN. Thank you. And I again want to thank the witnesses. Secretary Slater, I think it is one point here to—and I am sorry to belabor it but I will be quick. I worked very closely with you and worked very closely with Dr. Bailey's predecessor, on airbags and on a whole lot of other issues. Never once has any of you come to me and said, look. We have got to increase this budget. Be our advocate here. And so I just want to make it clear that not only have we not resisted any increases, I think this committee would have been very receptive to an increase in funding.

But that is behind us now. Let us work on this legislation. And let us also try and work together on seeing what additional funds that are necessary to prevent this from ever occurring again. And I think we have had a very excellent working relationship and one that I am very pleased with. But now it is a very important time that we really coordinate our efforts. It is not going to help anybody if we get in a disagreement between this committee and the administration in trying to enact this legislation within the next few weeks.

Secretary SLATER. Thank you, Mr. Chairman. You are absolutely correct.

The CHAIRMAN. Thank you, both. Thank you. Our next witness is Mr. Masatoshi Ono, the Chief Executive Officer of Bridgestone/Firestone of Tokyo, Japan. And obviously your full testimony will be made part of the record, Mr. Ono. But also take whatever time that you feel necessary with your opening comments. Welcome before the committee.

STATEMENT OF MASATOSHI ONO, CHIEF EXECUTIVE OFFICER, BRIDGESTONE/FIRESTONE, INC.

Mr. ONO. Chairman McCain and Senator Hollings and members of the Committee, as the Chief Executive Officer, I come before you to express my deep regret and the sympathy to you and the American people and especially to the families who have lost loved ones in these terrible auto accidents.

I also come to accept full and personal responsibility on behalf of Bridgestone/Firestone for the events that led to this hearing. Whenever people are hurt or fatally injured in automobile accidents, it is tragic. Whenever people are injured while riding on Firestone tires, it is cause for great concern among Bridgestone/Firestone management and our 35,000 American employees. We are committed to resolving this situation and regaining the trust of our customers. My experience last week suggested that my problems with English may have limited our ability to explain important issues to you and the American people. So I would ask that our remarks be completed by our Executive Vice President, Mr. John Lampe.

STATEMENT OF JOHN LAMPE, EXECUTIVE VICE PRESIDENT, ACCOMPANIED BY BOB WYANT, VICE PRESIDENT FOR QUALITY ASSURANCE, BRIDGESTONE/FIRESTONE, INC.

Mr. LAMPE. Mr. Chairman, Senator Hollings, members of the committee, with your permission, my name is John Lampe. I am an Executive Vice President with Bridgestone/Firestone.

We want to thank you for calling this hearing. Last month on August 9, our company announced a voluntary recall of over 14 million tires made over a 10-year period. We took this action out of concern for customer safety. We must and we do take full responsibility for the recalled tires and the things that we have done before August 9 and since.

I firmly believe that we have been and will continue to be open and honest in these hearings and with the American public. However, I know that we have not been successful in communicating our most basic message, that our company and the thousands of employees who make up our company have a true and deep concern for consumer safety and customer satisfaction.

We pledge to have open and transparent processes so that our customers, the Congress and the public can be confident that we have done the right thing now and will continue to do so in the future.

I also know that we make great tire products on which millions of Americans have driven for billions of safe miles. But at the same time, gentlemen, I recognize and we recognize there is a problem, a very complex problem that must be solved because lives are at stake. And for too long we did not see the problem.

The tire industry's traditional measures of product performance—test data, analysis of failed tires and warning adjustment data—told us that these tires were fine. And although we knew we had claims, and when we evaluated tires involved in these claims, we did not believe the statistics generated by those claims was a good indicator of tire performance and product performance.

We believed until recently that the accidents and claims reported were simply part of supplying a large number of vehicles like the SUVs and light trucks. Our feeling was that the large population and vehicle characteristics alone explained these accidents and that was wrong. Our own data ultimately demonstrated that.

In early August, with the assistance of Ford, a statistical analysis of our claim data was conducted that demonstrated that the tires are clearly part of the problem. When we fully understood this new analysis, we acted to get the tires off the road, even though we could not identify a cause or causes. We acted because each and every accident that causes serious injuries or death is devastating to us. And, Senator Frist, I am sorry for your loss as well, sir.

Tire failure is a result. We must now focus on the cause. We have been working day and night to try to determine the root cause or causes of the tire problem. And finding that cause is made much more difficult because we are looking at a very small percentage of failures in an extremely large population of tires. But we believe we have narrowed the focus and believe the solution may lie in two areas, the unique design specification of the size P235/75R15 combined with variations in the manufacturing process at the Decatur plant. We are appointing Dr. Sanjay Govindjee, an independent, outside, completely independent, third party investigator to verify our work to date and to help us move to a more definitive solution on the tire piece of the puzzle.

We take full responsibility, Senators, when a tire fails because of a defect. We firmly believe, however, that the tire is only part of the overall safety problem shown by these tragic accidents. If we are really concerned—and we are—about consumer safety, we will leave no stone unturned. There are other questions that still must be answered in this complex puzzle.

The entire issue of tire inflation pressures selected by the vehicle manufacturer must be addressed. Does it provide an adequate safety margin to guard against damage caused by underinflation and overloading?

For example, at PSI, at 26 pounds per square inch, the Ford Explorer has little safety margin to guard against overloading. That is one of the reasons that we have recommended 30 PSI for that vehicle. Problems can and do occur if the air pressure drops below the originally specified level.

So what margin of safety should be required? Tires will fail. Dr. Bailey said it. Tires will fail and they do fail for a number of reasons. But in most cases, while experiencing a tire failure, the driver can bring that automobile under safe control.

However, we have seen an alarming number of serious accidents from rollovers of SUVs after a tire failure. Federal data shows that there have been over 16,000 rollovers with the Ford Explorer causing 600 deaths. The tire failure has been involved in only a very, very small percentage of these deaths.

But since we know a tire can fail and no death is acceptable, is there a dynamic test that can minimize the role of the tire in such catastrophic events? We believe that in the interest to public safety, one of the areas of focus for future valuations by NHTSA, by us, by the automobile industry, should be the interaction between the tire and the vehicle.

The Senator has already talked about the Federal motor safety standards that were initiated in 1968. They do not address this vehicle population, a population which has exploded in the past 10 years. These issues have been difficult for us. We are not vehicle experts. And these issues may have made it harder for us to see that problems we had and that we now recognize in our tires. Or do we see the future?

First, the tire industry, the National Highway Traffic Safety Administration and the auto industry need to work together to immediately detect and address tire problems and vehicle problems. We fully support the National Highway Traffic Safety Administration on reporting of overseas information regarding tire safety, revisions to the tire safety standards, developing early warning systems to quickly identify failure trends, dynamic testing to identify those vehicles which have tendencies to roll over and to design ways to address this. We support in-vehicle low pressure warning systems.

We talk about inflation a lot. In-vehicle low pressure warning system. And we are in favor and would support increasing penalties for violations of safety laws and regulations. We also strongly believe in educating the public about the importance of tire maintenance. We have developed a comprehensive, multi-part program to better accomplish this which I can address in the questions and answers.

Senators we are committed to take every step necessary to address these problems. We pledge our cooperation with this committee and with NHTSA to work to ensure the safety of all motoring public. All of our employees are committed to this. We recently were able to come to a successful labor agreement with the United Steel Workers of America. The United Steel Workers of America, who are represented in this room today, and their members will support and will help us overcome and accomplish what we have to do.

As a tire manufacturer, we will continue to serve society with products of superior quality and work diligently to regain the trust of our customers. There are a lot of specifics, Senators, that I would have liked to have covered about the recall itself. But I am sure I will get the opportunity to do that in the question and answers.

I would close by saying mistakes can be and are tragic. It is even more tragic not to learn by our mistakes and to prevent them from happening in the future. Mr. Chairman, thank you very, very much. And we welcome any questions that you may have.

[The prepared statement of Mr. Ono follows:]

PREPARED STATEMENT OF MASATOSHI ONO, CHIEF EXECUTIVE OFFICER, BRIDGESTONE/FIRESTONE, INC.

Chairman McCain, Senator Hollings and Members of the Committee:

As Chief Executive Officer, I come before you to express my deep regret and sympathy to you, the American people and especially to the families who have lost loved ones in these terrible rollover accidents. I also come to accept full and personal responsibility on behalf of Bridgestone/Firestone for the events that led to this hearing. Whenever people are hurt or fatally injured in automobile accidents, it is tragic. Whenever people are injured while riding on Firestone tires, it is cause for great concern among Bridgestone/Firestone's management and our 35,000 American employees. We are committed to resolving this situation and regaining the trust of our customers.

My experience last week suggested that my problems with English may have limited our ability to explain important issues to you and the American people. I would ask that our remarks be completed by our executive vice president, Mr. John Lampe.

PREPARED STATEMENT OF JOHN LAMPE, EXECUTIVE VICE PRESIDENT, BRIDGESTONE/FIRESTONE, INC.

Chairman McCain, Senator Hollings, and Members of this Committee:

We want to thank you for calling this hearing. It has been a new experience for us to be appearing before Congress, and probably for any company to be subject to such an intense Congressional investigation as has occurred over such a short period of time. But, we are greatly benefiting from this process to learn about our own mistakes, and to work with you, Members of the Committee, toward ensuring that our tires and all tires are as safe as possible.

Firestone has manufactured hundreds of millions of safe tires for over one hundred years. Americans have driven billions of safe miles on safe Firestone tires. That is why this situation, with deaths and serious injuries, must be addressed and should never happen again.

It is little more than a month ago, on August 8, that we met with the National Highway Traffic and Safety Administration and together reviewed the performance of tires that have been associated with tread separations. These accidents have primarily occurred on the Ford Explorer vehicle. We regret that almost 10% of those rollovers involved tire separations. In light of that fact, we announced a voluntary safety recall of 6.5 million tires.

We are recalling those tires as quickly as possible. We are making every effort to determine why certain tires failed. So far, we have replaced 2 million tires. Although we sped up production, we cannot meet full demand. To help alleviate that problem, we are paying for competitor tires to act as replacements. We are reviewing every aspect of our manufacturing and control processes. We are making microscopic examinations of many recalled tires.

We also are trying to work with Ford Motor Company to understand the cause. This has led us to understand a key point for the future. The government and others have tended to look at auto safety and tire safety separately. We believe that it is important to look at both issues together. Correct tires must be matched with vehicles; the mutual duties of tire manufacturers and automobile manufacturers must be made absolutely clear. If only it were possible to find a simple cause, such as certain tires made at a certain time and a certain plant, we would have resolved the problem.

But, we cannot today provide you with a conclusive cause of our past problems. We will not rest until we determine the cause.

We wish to take this opportunity to clarify some key points that were raised at last week's hearings.

- First, why didn't we immediately alert NHTSA and the American public when incidents involving rollovers occurred in Saudi Arabia?
- Second, why didn't we act on claims data and immediately recall our tires?
- Third, did we encourage Ford to conceal information from NHTSA relating to what occurred in Saudi Arabia?
- Fourth, did Ford have to "pry" information out of us relevant to potentially serious or fatal injuries as a result of rollover accidents?
- Fifth, are we going to make an additional recall of the 1.4 million tires suggested by NHTSA?
- Sixth, what speed tests did we conduct or not conduct, and why?
- Seventh, what information have we learned about what went wrong at our Decatur plant in 1995 and 1996?

We will provide this Committee our best answers to these crucial questions.

Perhaps left out of the klieg lights of last week's hearings, which focused on matters of the past, was the actions we will take now to assure the American public that Firestone tires are safe.

First, we will appoint an outside, independent investigator to assist in tire analysis and determine the root cause of the tire problem. This investigator will help assure you and the American public that Firestone tires are reliable now and in the future.

Second, we will fully cooperate with this Committee about tire safety. We will release data and information in order to assure consumer safety with our products.

Third, we are accelerating a rollout of a nationwide consumer education program. If there is any good that has come out of this very bad situation, it is the need for the American people to be fully informed about tire safety. Our education program will take place in almost 7,000 company stores and Firestone dealers. It will provide everyone with information about proper tire maintenance and safety. We will use in-store videos, showroom displays, brochures, windshield tire pressure reminders, and tire pressure gauges. We will strive to assure that all consumers understand the safe use of tires.

Fourth, we pledge to continue to work with NHTSA toward developing better "early warning systems" about tire safety. We commend NHTSA Administrator Bailey for her suggestions. We will inform NHTSA about recalls that occur in foreign countries. We will work with NHTSA to develop an in-vehicle system to alert drivers about tire pressure.

Fifth, we will work with this committee to develop any necessary legislative remedies that will assure to the American public that their tires and vehicles are safe. The distinct roles of tire and vehicle manufacturers regarding safety need to be brought together, rather than looked at separately. We will work with you to bring this disconnect to an end.

With us today are some leaders of our union workers. We stand united as we work together to assure millions of families that have put their trust and faith in Firestone that, now and in the future, we will manufacture the safe tires that every consumer can trust. Mistakes can be tragic, but it is more tragic not to learn from them. We will work with you in this hearing and in the future to achieve that goal.

The CHAIRMAN. Thank you, Mr. Lampe. For the record, would you state your formal relationship with Bridgestone/Firestone?

Mr. LAMPE. Yes, sir. I am an Executive Vice President with Bridgestone/Firestone. And my specific responsibilities are I am in charge and responsible for our sales in the after market, not to OE, but in the after market. And, Senator McCain, may I ask that we be joined, if we may, by Bob Wyant who is our Vice President for Quality Assurance?

The CHAIRMAN. He would be welcome. Mr. Wyant, if you would like to.

Mr. WYANT. Thank you, Senator.

The CHAIRMAN. Take a seat at the table. My first question is Bridgestone/Firestone has repeatedly stated that it was not aware of a problem with the tires subject to recall until August of this year. However, in a September 9, 2000, article, *The Washington Post* reported an ample documentation existed of multiple warnings to your company of a possible defect, including a mid-1998 report that showed a dramatic increase in customer claims relating to tread separation in the tires that are now subject to recall.

Additionally, annual Firestone reports on claims data indicated a dramatic increase in claims in 1998 and 1999. Did not the increased number of claims in conjunction with the problems you were having overseas give you some indication that you were having a problem?

Mr. LAMPE. Senator McCain, I think it is very important that I start off by explaining when we talk about claims because there will be a lot of questions on claims. Claims for us and for NHTSA are represented really by three different distinct pieces. One is product damage claims. And that makes up the overwhelming majority of the total claims number when we look at that. We also have personal injuries and we also have lawsuits.

Senator McCain, I would like to address the property damage part of that. It is the overwhelming piece of numbers. Senator McCain, our business—and I guess I have to say the support from our customers over the last 7 years—has been overwhelming. We have actually doubled, more than doubled, our sales in the last 6 years. We would have expected our claims numbers in absolute numbers to rise. We would have expected the dollar amount of our property damage claims to arise. But, Senator, the mistake we made is that we never used claims data as an indicator of tire performance.

The CHAIRMAN. Why not?

Mr. LAMPE. We used—and we do not have any excuses other than to say we used the traditional and the more approved, proven methods that I believe the industry uses. And I cannot speak for everybody. But we use things like adjustment data, tires coming in that we see and we touch. We use field surveys to go out actually to the field. We used testing. We used those because they were traditional. And then all of a sudden, we have this claims information. And when we did this analysis with—believe me—with the help of Ford—Ford did most of the analysis—we see that it clearly pointed out that we had some problems in certain areas.

The CHAIRMAN. Ford executives allege that they became suspicious of a potential problem with Bridgestone/Firestone tires in foreign markets and that Ford requested data that you may have then possessed confirming their suspicion. They say that in response you only provided warranty adjustment data which showed no sign of problems, and not claims data, which would have indicated a problem. Is that true?

Mr. LAMPE. Senator McCain, we have supplied Ford over the years any technical data, engineering data, that they have requested. Ford never requested, to the best of my knowledge—and we have had this conversation within my company—Ford never requested claims data until the middle of this year, June or July. We had been requested by NHTSA to supply that claims data as well. We were putting it together for NHTSA. We supplied it to NHTSA in July. And within 2 to 3 weeks after that, we supplied it to Ford. I have absolutely no knowledge of any requests for claims data prior to that from Ford.

The CHAIRMAN. My time has expired. Senator Hollings.

Senator HOLLINGS. That has to do with the claims. How about lawsuits? I notice now you will inform NHTSA about the recalls that occur in foreign countries. What is the position now of Bridgestone/Firestone on the actual lawsuits? You are right. A lot of these claims are with respect to the warranty. But when you get a lawsuit, you have got usually property damage, injury, maybe a death.

Mr. LAMPE. Yes, sir.

Senator HOLLINGS. Will you also go along with notifying us about the lawsuits? Because that to me rather than seal the records and not let anybody know which they claim the lawyers or the judges or the system requires or allows. What about you yourself, Bridgestone/Firestone? Would you go along with us now in letting us have the information with respect to lawsuits?

Mr. LAMPE. One hundred percent, Senator Hollings. And let me do mention, there has been one of the Senators in the opening remarks talked about gag orders. And I need to explain this. We have never, ever asked for a gag order on any trial proceedings or litigation unless it involved trade secrets which does require a Judge to issue a formal court order. And when he does that, we ask for protection on trade secrets, and the amount of settlement between the two parties. That is the only thing that we have ever asked for, confidentiality on litigation. And we have supplied all of that information to NHTSA. And we will to you, Senator Hollings.

Senator HOLLINGS. Are you saying the claimant's attorney is the one that has been requesting that?

Mr. LAMPE. No, sir. I am not saying that at all. I am not saying that at all.

Senator HOLLINGS. That crowd loves publicity.

Mr. LAMPE. I am not saying that at all.

Senator HOLLINGS. They get a big verdict or a big settlement, you cannot keep their mouth shut at the club. That is all you hear about for a week. Well, who is claiming that we ought to have the gag order? Not the judge.

Mr. LAMPE. No, sir. No, sir. Please, I will explain. We have asked for confidentiality on only two things in all of our litigation. One is trade secrets. And one is the amount of settlements. Sometimes that is our request. Sometimes it is a joint request by the plaintiff.

But we have supplied all that information and will continue to supply that information with the plaintiff's admission to NHTSA and to the hearings, believe me, sir.

Senator HOLLINGS. Now, we have had some 88 deaths, 250 injuries. And you take a whole paragraph of your statement here, a third, that we will strive to assure that all consumers understand the safe use of tires. Intimating, of course, that there has been some unsafe use of tires. Can you tell me in the 88 deaths or 250 injuries the example of the unsafe use of tires?

Mr. LAMPE. Senator Hollings, and please the rest of the Senators, we are not trying to blame the public. We do believe that we should as an industry have been doing a better job on educating the public. Tire maintenance, Senator Hollings, is extremely important, extremely important. Tire inflation is critical, critical, to the performance and the durability of the tire.

Senator HOLLINGS. Is there some dispute about that inflation, that should have been in these rollover deaths or claims or injuries? Is there a difference between you and Ford with respect to that tire pressure?

Mr. LAMPE. Sir, when the original tire pressure was established and it was selected by the manufacturer, we as a tire manufacturer agreed with that inflation pressure. And we started to see some——

Senator HOLLINGS. What was that?

Mr. LAMPE. It was on the Ford Explorer specifically, sir. It was 26 pounds front and rear. When we began to see, looking at the claims data, the number of incidents, the number of rollovers and so forth, we went to Ford and told them that we would like to recommend 30 pounds of air pressure which we think give a better safety margin. And Ford did agree to have a range of inflation between 26 and 30 pounds.

Senator HOLLINGS. Thank you, Mr. Chairman.

The CHAIRMAN. Thank you, sir. Senator Snowe.

Senator SNOWE. Thank you, Mr. Chairman. Mr. Lampe, does Firestone still maintain that the defective tires are essentially manufactured in Decatur's plant?

Mr. LAMPE. I am sorry, Senator Snowe. That the defective tires are manufactured——

Senator SNOWE. Right.

Mr. LAMPE. There were two sets, two parts, of the recalled tires, Senator Snowe. One was ATX's that were produced in a number of plants primarily in Decatur, but in a number of plants. Those are all being recalled. And then specifically, the Wilderness AT that was produced in the Decatur plant is also part of that being recalled.

Senator SNOWE. There are a number of plants involved.

Mr. LAMPE. In the ATX, the older tires, yes, ma'am.

Senator SNOWE. A report that was issued yesterday indicated the Wilderness tires that the tread separation increased 194 percent between 1998 and 1999. Is that something that your company would have been aware of at the time?

Mr. LAMPE. Yes, it should have been—it was something that our company was aware of at the time. Again, and it is hard to put it in perspective unless we measure—and I wish I had that information for you. And I will provide it for you. If we could measure and show you the amount of separations on the Wilderness compared to our sales or compared to our production, that line, that Wilderness line, was introduced in 1996. It is one of the biggest lines we have ever made and sold. It went on the Ford Explorer. It is a huge population of tires. For our absolute numbers to have increased 196 percent to me does not say anything if we do not compare it to what the population was. And I will get you that information.

Senator SNOWE. How do fatalities figure into that decision-making with respect to tread separation?

Mr. LAMPE. Fatalities are a tragedy. One is not acceptable. One is not acceptable. And we had individual cases of fatalities that we looked at. We examined the tire. We did everything we could to make sure that tire did not have a problem that could have contributed to that. But obviously, Senator Snowe, as I said, we have made some bad tires. And we take full responsibility for that.

Senator SNOWE. It was indicated in one story that more than 4 years before Firestone gave Ford Motor Company or Federal regulators any hint of a problem with its tires for sport utility vehicles, the company's engineers had been alerted by the State of Arizona that their tire treads tended to separate in hot weather.

Mr. LAMPE. Senator McCain, I thought you might be interested in the State of Arizona. You want me to write the answer?

The CHAIRMAN. And I am also interested in salvaging my tattered voting record. So I will be back.

Mr. LAMPE. We can repeat the answer for Senator McCain. Yes, there was in 1996, Senator Snowe, there was a request by the Fish and Game Department or Wildlife and Park Department in Arizona to come out and look at a number of tires that they were not happy with. We did go out and we surveyed a number of tires. We sent out six engineers. Senator Snowe, in the case of—in the 1996 case, we found many, many passenger tires, regular passenger service tires on their vehicles which as their name would imply, Wildlife and Parks, were used in much off the road conditions. We went through a number of tires and found not one tire, not one tire, that had a defect that would have been adjusted. The tire was not proper for the application. We took those tires off. We gave them credit. And they used that credit to buy a special service truck tire from us to put on their vehicle. I do not believe that the 1996 thing had anything to do with—to the best of my recollection of what I've been informed—has nothing to do with tread separation.

Senator SNOWE. Has the company responded to NHTSA's requests for all of the documents?

Mr. LAMPE. Yes, ma'am. It has. And I heard Dr. Bailey mention that she does not have the Arizona document. And I have made a note. And I will commit to you and the committee that if she does not have that, if that was not in our submission, that we will get that information—if that information is available, we will get that to her.

Senator SNOWE. So the company's not withholding any documents that have been requested by NHTSA.

Mr. LAMPE. Absolutely not, Senator Snowe.

Senator SNOWE. None whatsoever.

Mr. LAMPE. Absolutely not.

Senator SNOWE. So it is not necessary for them to use their subpoena power?

Mr. LAMPE. Absolutely not, Senator Snowe.

Senator SNOWE. Thank you.

Senator BRYAN. Thank you very much, Senator. Let me try to get a handle on the term, "We made some bad tires." I believe that is the language you used, Mr. Lampe. Am I correct on that?

Mr. LAMPE. Yes, Senator.

Senator BRYAN. And are bad tires to be equated with tires that have defects of some kind?

Mr. LAMPE. Yes, sir.

Senator BRYAN. Now, what tires do you acknowledge have defects?

Mr. LAMPE. Sir, we made a very small percentage of tires in our Decatur facility with the Wilderness AT that we believe could pose a safety problem.

Senator BRYAN. Now, are the ATX, the ATXII, different than the Wilderness tires? We have been led to believe that there may be some difference. Help us to understand what we are talking about.

Mr. LAMPE. Yes, sir. The ATX—and I am sorry, the whole ATX, ATXII thing got confused. We only have one tire, the ATX. We at one point in time changed the designation internally for ATXII, but it still says ATX on the tire. So there is really one tire. That tire was introduced in mid- or late 1980's and was produced and supplied as original equipment up through 1995 and the beginning of 1996. It was discontinued for original equipment, replaced by the Wilderness. We did continue to produce smaller amounts of the ATX in our plants for the replacement market.

Senator BRYAN. So again, ATX and ATXII are one and the same tire.

Mr. LAMPE. ATX and ATXII are one and the same tire, sir.

Senator BRYAN. And Wilderness, that would be a separate tire run? Is that correct?

Mr. LAMPE. Yes, the Wilderness AT was a separate tire.

Senator BRYAN. So we are really dealing with two different tires.

Mr. LAMPE. Two different tires, one size.

Senator BRYAN. Now, do you acknowledge that there are defects in the Wilderness tires?

Mr. LAMPE. Sir, we acknowledge safety problems and defects in a very small percentage of the Wilderness tires that were produced in Decatur, yes sir.

Senator BRYAN. So there is some agreement that there are defects in the ATX and the Wilderness tires.

Mr. LAMPE. Yes, Senator.

Senator BRYAN. Now, safety advocates have urged that there be a recall of all of these tires in light of the uncertainties and the concern of the public. Let me just say people are really frightened, Mr. Lampe. They have read these articles. They have seen television accounts. They know generally that people have died as a result of problems and others have received injuries on an ongoing basis. Would it not be the corporate responsible thing to do to simply issue a recall of all of these tires, both the 15 inch as well as the 16 inch.

Mr. LAMPE. Sir, I would not think that—I do not believe that would be responsible. And, sir, I think it would be counterproductive to be replacing good tires with good tires. Right now we have a task ahead of us to replace 6.5 million tires. We have only replaced two million. I say only even though it has been a month. We have four million tires to replace. Anything that would interfere with that task before us to replace those four million tires to me, sir, would be an injustice.

Senator BRYAN. And so it is Bridgestone/Firestone's position that they are not going to expand the recall.

Mr. LAMPE. At this time, no sir.

Senator BRYAN. Now, I think I understood you to say, and correct me if I'm wrong, Mr. Lampe, that you first became aware of the defects in July of this year? If I have mischaracterized your testimony, let me make sure that I give you an opportunity to correct my statement. I thought I understood you to say, if I heard you incorrectly, tell me when you first became aware of the defects.

Mr. LAMPE. Sir, we first became aware of the safety problem when Ford analyzed our claims data, statistically analyzed it. And they spent a lot of time and a lot of resources to do this.

Senator BRYAN. And when was that?

Mr. LAMPE. This was to the best of my recollection, sir, it was early August. Early August.

Senator BRYAN. Of this year.

Mr. LAMPE. Of this year, sir.

Senator BRYAN. Well, I think what we find so incredulous about that is that we have had a whole series of recalls beginning in Saudi Arabia in 1999 in August. Let me ask you in terms of knowledge, were you aware of those recalls that occurred in August 1999 in Saudi Arabia?

Mr. WYANT. Might I answer that question?

Senator BRYAN. Yes. I think the answer could be yes or no. If you did not know, that is fine. But, yes sir. Mr. Wyant, I think it is. Were you aware of that?

Mr. WYANT. The Saudi Arabia action was known to us. We in fact had joint studies.

Senator BRYAN. Again, my time is limited. So the answer would be yes, sir, that you did know about the recall.

Mr. WYANT. Yes.

Senator BRYAN. And that was August 1999. And again, I take it that you may have been aware then of the Malaysia, Thailand, Venezuela, Columbia, Ecuador recalls all of which predated the August, 2000 recall notice here in the United States. Would that be correct as well?

Mr. WYANT. Well, first of all, these customer actions were actually generated by the Ford Motor Company.

Senator BRYAN. I understand that. But, Mr. Wyant, we are trying to get the facts. I mean, you were aware of it.

Mr. WYANT. Yes.

Senator BRYAN. So as the lawyers would say, you would be charged with—there was a whole series of recalls, whether you did it or Ford did it, but these tires are being recalled. And you did have knowledge of each of these I take it.

Mr. WYANT. We had knowledge of these, but very limited knowledge in the Malaysia area. But the other two, we had knowledge. And those actions on the part of Ford were because of the local service conditions.

Mr. LAMPE. Senator Bryan, we were aware that Ford was making a customer satisfaction exchange.

Senator BRYAN. Well, let me just simply say that I think I would charge you with notice that there is a serious problem. There are a half a dozen countries that are involved here. And what we find to be troublesome, and I want to give you an opportunity to respond. You are all aware of this Ford memorandum that has been produced which would indicate if true—and we want to get your response to this—that at the time these recalls were being discussed, Firestone objected because they were concerned that to issue such a recall would impose upon them a burden to notify U.S. DOT or NHTSA. Now, the clear inference of that is that you were trying to conceal and hide this information.

This is Ford's memo. Let me understand what your interpretation of your actions are.

Mr. WYANT. Senator, that particular notification that you read dealt with an engineering judgment in Saudi Arabia. After the surveys and analysis of the data and these extreme conditions in Saudi Arabia, it was an engineering judgment that there was not a tire defect involved with it.

Second, the conversation that you referred to with conversation in our organization to the sales company that that was an issue that should be discussed. That was not a warning sign or anything of that sort to the Ford Motor Company.

Mr. LAMPE. Senator Bryan, if I may too, just one quick comment to point out.

Senator BRYAN. Yes.

Mr. LAMPE. The survey that we did in Saudi Arabia, we did it jointly with Ford. And it was jointly agreed that the tires in Saudi Arabia that we were looking at were failing—the ones we saw were failing due to the extreme conditions—extreme conditions. And that was agreed upon with Ford.

Senator BRYAN. Mr. Lampe, I guess the question did Bridgestone/Firestone agree that the tires should be recalled?

Mr. LAMPE. No, sir. We did not.

Senator BRYAN. They did not. So Ford took a position with which you disagree.

Mr. LAMPE. Yes, sir.

Senator BRYAN. And is that true with respect to the other recalls that we have in Malaysia, Thailand, Venezuela, Columbia and Ecuador?

Mr. WYANT. We have no knowledge of the basis of that in that—well, in the Malaysia, Thailand area, we had very limited information. We did have some knowledge of it certainly. But I do not know the basis of that particular action. In the Venezuela arena, they did take action similar, I believe, to what was taken in Saudi Arabia.

Senator BRYAN. Would it be correct to assume that in some instances you are saying you had no knowledge with respect to Venezuela? You did not know the date upon which they based it. But in any event, you did not affirmatively as a company concur or agree with the recalls in these other countries.

Mr. WYANT. That's correct.

Senator BRYAN. Well, I mean, you have got a company like Ford Motor Company? They are in business to make a profit. And that is not a dirty word in America. Would that not suggest to you that if they were initiating these recalls, that we have got now several countries that you were aware of. Does that not elevate or heighten your concern that, "Hey? We may have a problem here?"

Mr. WYANT. Senator, I am trying to clarify that in those two arenas, Saudi Arabia and Venezuela, we did not participate because there was no indication of a tire defect.

Senator BRYAN. I understand you didn't participate. But that is not my question. My question is that Ford Motor Company decided to recall those tires. They do not just do that without some great reason for doing so, one has to conclude. My point is does that not place the company with some affirmative responsibility to say, "wait a minute if Ford is recalling these tires, even though we may not disagree, we have got a real problem here."

Mr. WYANT. Sir, due to the local conditions, there is always the question of "Is this an appropriate tire?" The tires that were removed from the market, are those appropriate tires for that market? And that is part of the consideration or issue that Ford has to deal with.

Senator BRYAN. But I take it that these tires were sold in American markets, am I correct? The tires that were sold in Saudi Arabia. The tires that were sold in Venezuela that you acknowledge that you had some knowledge of. Those were the same tires that were sold in the U.S. were they not?

Mr. WYANT. The Venezuelan situation, the tires there that were from the U.S. market were extremely small.

Senator BRYAN. Not the same tires.

Mr. WYANT. Pardon?

Senator BRYAN. Not the same tires then.

Mr. WYANT. Most of those tires are actually produced in Venezuela for the local Venezuelan market.

Senator BRYAN. But, Mr. Wyant, I think, you know, let us not go into these nuances. Are they the same tires or not? If they are not the same tires, then we have got a different situation. It is not a question of where they are produced. Are they the same tires, the ATXs or ATXII, which I understand is one and the same, the Wilderness, are those the same tires that were being sold in the U.S.?

Mr. WYANT. In the case of Venezuela, they are not the same tires.

Senator BRYAN. They are not the same tires. How about Saudi Arabia?

Mr. WYANT. In Saudi Arabia, the tires and vehicles were exported to Saudi Arabia and they are USA produced tires.

Senator BRYAN. My point being we do live on one planet. I happen to come from a State, as does our distinguished Chairman, in which we get temperatures in the summertime that very closely approximate the kind of driving conditions that one would have in Saudi Arabia. My point being it strikes me that we had some affirmative obligation on your part. I know we have gone into this.

My last question, Mr. Chairman, because I am going to have to slip away and vote too, is you have indicated, I think, Mr. Wyant, that you have provided all documents that NHTSA has requested. My question is a little different. Are you prepared at this point to disclose all documents, memos, correspondence, any type of communication, that you have had either internally with Ford or any other company, or with your customers that you have in your corporate files?

Mr. WYANT. That is certainly correct. If I may clarify one issue if you will, sir.

Senator BRYAN. Yes.

Mr. WYANT. Particularly on the Saudi Arabia situation, I do not believe that those conditions of operation there are comparable to the United States. It is common practice in Saudi Arabia to let substantial amounts of air out of your tires when you go out into the desert. And there is not too much availability of air when you come back in. There is also substantial puncture. And there are tire failures, substantial tire failures, in that environment. But the environment is much more severe than it is in the United States.

Mr. LAMPE. Senator Bryan, to answer your question, we will make all documents available to NHTSA.

Senator BRYAN. And will you do so voluntarily?

Mr. LAMPE. Yes, sir.

Senator BRYAN. In other words, it is not a question of whether or not the question is precisely asked. You are saying any document, any kind of correspondence, memorandum, you will make that available and do so. And would you also make that available to the Committee?

Mr. LAMPE. Yes, Senator.

Senator BRYAN. And I thank you very much, Mr. Lampe, Mr. Wyant, Mr. Ono. Thank you, Mr. Chairman.

The CHAIRMAN. Thank you, Senator Bryan. You wanted to tell me about Arizona.

Mr. LAMPE. The question was asked as you were leaving, Senator, about Arizona. There was a report that in 1996, we had a request from one of the government agencies in Arizona—I think it was the Arizona Parks and Recreations Department—to come out and take a look at some tires that they were not happy with. We went out, surveyed the tires. We sent out six engineers and found that the majority of the vehicles were using passenger, normal passenger type, product. Even though they did a lot of off the road and fairly heavy service type duty. We examined the tires, did not find one single tire that would be adjustable under material defect or workmanship. But we went ahead and we replaced the tires. We gave credit to the department. And they turned around and used that credit to buy heavy duty special service tires from us for their vehicles. And that was the 1996 Parks and Recreations Department event.

The CHAIRMAN. Well, I thank you for that. I think that many automobile owners in Arizona who were using Bridgestone/Firestone tires would have liked to have known about your recall in Saudi Arabia as well. I thank you for appearing. Senator Wyden.

Senator WYDEN. Thank you, Mr. Chairman. I appreciate it. My apologies to the witnesses since we had a vote. One followup question if I might, Mr. Lampe. You told Senator Hollings that Firestone only seeks confidentiality for trade secrets and the size of the verdicts. Therefore, would Firestone support a requirement that NHTSA be notified of lawsuit settlements involving claims of safety problems with your tires?

Mr. LAMPE. Yes, Senator. We would.

Senator WYDEN. Question for Mr. Ono if I might. And I understand that we have assistance for this. Mr. Ono, only about 2 million of the 6.5 million tires covered by the recall have now been replaced. So there is a recall that has been going on for a month now. Do you find it acceptable that after a month we still have potentially millions of tires that may be deadly still on the roads?

Mr. ONO. As far as replacing two million tires in 1 month, I am not satisfied with that. We have doubled the production capacity of our factories domestically. And we have—that is over the production level at the beginning of August. And also, we have doubled the production of tires in Japan so that customers can receive the replacement tires. We are airlifting tires from Japan. So we are doing all that we can. And there is no precedence to this, but in our industry we are having customers replace their tires with our competitors' tires such as Goodyear, General and Michelin.

Mr. LAMPE. Senator Wyden, if I could, sir. I think the point about the competitors' tires, it was after the recall was announced when certainly we knew we did not have enough local production on our own and Mr. Ono asked me the next day after August 10 in fact to contact our competitors. And I personally contacted a number of our major competitors who were very supportive, and increased their production tremendously on this size. And we can avail ourselves to the competitor tires as well.

Senator WYDEN. Well, I will say, as I did in my opening statement, I'm especially concerned about this. My State is one of those in the rear with respect to the recall. And Oregonians are very troubled about the prospect that it may be well into next year. It is just critically important to me that this be expedited. I want to hear about a time table that is considerably sped up.

Mr. LAMPE. Senator Wyden, I agree with you. But believe me, Oregon is not being snubbed. We started replacing tires in every state the day we made the announcement. We did not say that we were going to do these states and these states and these states. All we said was we were going to try to prioritize some of the production for the states that had the highest incidence. You, Senator, are very fortunate. You have a very large, very successful dealer in Oregon. And in Washington, Senator Gorton had the same question. Les Schwab, who has told us last week that he alone—he alone—in his stores has changed over 120,000 tires just that one dealership. So I think we are making good progress. Is it good enough? It will never be good enough, Senator. But good progress in the State of Oregon.

Senator WYDEN. Because I was out of the room, I am not sure if this question was raised. But, as you know, the newspapers this morning talked about significant management changes in the United States with respect to Firestone. Can you tell us any more about what is going to be pursued in that area?

Mr. LAMPE. Senator, I cannot. I read that myself this morning and I will have to get back to my office just to make sure it is still there.

Senator WYDEN. Mr. Chairman, thank you.

The CHAIRMAN. Thank you. Thank you for appearing before the Committee today.

Mr. LAMPE. Thank you, Senator McCain.

The CHAIRMAN. Now we would like to hear from Mr. Jac Nasser who is the Chief Executive Officer of Ford Motor Company. Mr. Nasser, thank you for your patience. I apologize for the breaks required by roll call votes. Your complete statement will be made part of the record. But please take as much time as you wish to illuminate the committee. Welcome.

STATEMENT OF JAC NASSER, CHIEF EXECUTIVE OFFICER, FORD MOTOR COMPANY

Mr. NASSER. Thank you, very much. Good afternoon, Chairman McCain, Senator Hollings, and Members of the Committee. I appreciate this opportunity to update you and the American people on the Firestone tire recall. But before I discuss the Firestone tire recall, I would like to say a brief word about the Ford Motor Company if I may.

Ford Motor Company is a company that throughout its history has in its strength been its employees and its customers. I have been with the Ford Motor Company for over thirty years. I started as a trainee in Fort Australia. And I am honored to lead this company into the 21st Century as we look after our customers going forward.

I think as we have heard this morning in particular and last week, you and the public have questions regarding the Firestone recall. I am here to answer those questions. And I will remain here until the Committee is satisfied.

We have had some good discussion this morning. And I think it did get to the heart of the issue. And that is when did people know there was a problem with the Firestone tires? What have we done about it so far? And where are we heading in the future? And I appreciate the comments from many of the Senators who really concentrated on what do we all do collectively going forward?

Let us start with when did Ford know that there was a problem with the Firestone tires. I think it is worth repeating that because tires are the only component of any vehicle that are separately warranted, Ford did not know that there was a defect with the tires until we virtually pried the claims data from Firestone's hands in late July, early August, and analyzed it ourselves.

It was only then—and that was only a few days before the recall was announced—that Ford engineers found conclusive evidence at that point that the tires were defective. We then demanded that Firestone pull the tires from the road.

I must say that as we look back, the first signs of this problem developed in Saudi Arabia when our dealers reported complaints about certain Firestone tires. At that time, we immediately asked Firestone to investigate. Firestone did so. And they told us that the tread separations were caused by improper maintenance and road hazards. And I think you heard some of that earlier in the discussions with the Committee. And they said that those particular complaints were unique to that environment.

At that point, we weren't convinced by those explanations. So we asked Firestone to conduct additional tests on the tires. And I must say that after each and every test, Firestone reported that there was no defect in the tires. This did not satisfy our Saudi customers. So we replaced the tires about a year ago.

I should add that at about the same time, we wanted to know if our U.S. customers were having similar tire problems. And earlier last year, we asked Firestone to review its U.S. data in general. And we were assured by Firestone that there was no problem in this country regarding Firestone tires.

When he went back, our data, the government safety data and you heard from Mr. Slater and Ms. Bailey this morning, did not show anything either. Despite this, we asked Firestone for one more test. And Firestone examined tires in a special study in Texas, Nevada and Arizona. And they reported back as before that there was no defect to be found.

As you know, contrary to those repeated assurances, we later learned a very different story from Firestone's confidential claims data. And when we did, at that point in August of this year, we insisted that Firestone recall the defective tires.

Although I take no personal or professional pleasure in saying it, Firestone failed to share critical claims data with Ford that might have prompted the recall of these bad tires sooner. And I should say that last week I listened in disbelief as senior Firestone executives not only acknowledged that Firestone had analyzed its claims data, but also identified significant pattern of tread separations as early as 1998.

Yet, Firestone said nothing to anyone, including the Ford Motor Company. This is not the candid and frank dialog that Ford expects in its business relationships. And after Firestone's testimony last week, we expressed Ford's profound disappointment to the head of Bridgestone/Firestone in Japan.

It has been said before this morning, my purpose is not to finger point, but simply to tell you that at each step Ford took the initiative to uncover this problem and find a solution. We agree that we—everyone—needs to do a better job in this area. And looking back if I have one regret, looking back on all of this, it is that we did not ask Firestone the right questions sooner.

What have we done so far? As I said earlier, we started by insisting that Firestone recall the bad tires. And to encourage and even prod Firestone to take immediate action, Ford offered to share the cost of the recall. And we also requested the use of competitors' tires.

I then made a public commitment to our customers that Ford would dedicate its resources to support the Firestone recall. And in just 4 weeks—this is probably one of the fastest recalls in history—in just 4 weeks, over two million tires have been replaced. And we have worked very closely together with the rest of the global tire industry to increase tire availability.

As mentioned earlier, we shutdown production at three Ford plants to free up replacement tires that can be sent to our dealers for our customers. And just days ago, I extended the shutdown to free up even more replacement tires. This is all encouraging, but it is not good enough because we need to look forward.

And what do we need to do as we go forward? Mr. Chairman, there are almost three million Goodyear tires on Ford Explorers that have not had a tread separation problem here in the U.S. market. And data compiled by the Department of Transportation shows that the Explorer has a safety record that is second to none, particularly when you compare it to the average passenger car and competitive sports utility vehicle.

So based on these facts, and that's what we need to be driven by here, based on these facts, we know that this is a Firestone tire issue, not a vehicle issue. But regardless, we have got to all prevent this from happening again.

Last week, I announced that Ford would develop an early warning reporting system with tire companies that provides information on real world performance of tires. Since last week, we have actively pursued this particular idea with our tire suppliers and we have been very encouraged by their reaction.

I also announced that Ford would provide the Federal safety agency and its counterparts in other countries information on our safety actions around the world. And we will do this in advance of legislation that is pending. And from this point forward, when we know something, so will the world in terms of safety defects.

In addition, this was mentioned also earlier, I have requested that Ford's product development experts look into the feasibility of a dashboard indicator for future models which would alert customers to a potential tire problem. I can also announce to you today that later this year, beginning with our new Explorer, we will offer our customers a choice of tires.

Mr. Chairman, I want you and our customers to know that we at Ford will not rest until every bad tire is replaced. And I will do everything in my power as President of the Ford Motor Company to maintain the confidence and trust of our customers. Thank you. And I would be pleased to answer any questions at this time.

The CHAIRMAN. Thank you, Mr. Nasser. According to a *New York Times* article yesterday, Ford was informed of this problem as early as September 1998 by one of its own executives in a memo detailing problems with tread separation, Saudi Arabia, Oman, Venezuela. Then there was another memo—written by an executive in Venezuela, January 12, 1999 that suggests Ford officials in that country were aware of the problem of Firestone tires shedding their tread and causing accidents. The existence of these memos raises questions about when Ford Motor Company knew of this problem. I would like you to respond to that.

Mr. NASSER. Mr. Chairman, let me take the Middle East market and Venezuela because they are very different. They are different tires, different markets, different vehicles. In Venezuela, a very confused situation. Seventy-five percent of the tires in Venezuela are locally manufactured. They are a different tire as Firestone had indicated. There was mislabeling of tires, tires that did not meet the appropriate specification. And in Venezuela, the accident data base is very, very poor.

Despite all of that, we found that there were problems in terms of the Firestone tires. And we wanted Firestone to come along with us in terms of a recall. And they refused to do so. We went ahead because we knew there was a particular problem around the Venezuelan situation and the defects of those tires made in Venezuela. It had nothing to do with what was going on in the U.S. market.

In Saudi Arabia, these were 16 inch tires. And they were on a variety of vehicles. Test after test we did together with Firestone and independently. And in every case, when we went through and asked the question what was going on in the Saudi market, we at the same time went back and asked Firestone to check the U.S. data, every time, including the——

The CHAIRMAN. So you are saying you knew about it and you did something about it.

Mr. NASSER. Not only did we do something about it, but we actually examined all the data. And perhaps now is a good time to look at if you could look at the shot that is on Firestone tires in the U.S., that is the one that shows the cross hatches in terms of the bar. What this chart shows is that the number of reports of tread separations on a variety of Firestone tires—and it is based on the claims data that we received from Firestone on July the 28th of the year.

And if you look at the cross hatch which is the longest bar, the worst tires are the ATX tires produced at Decatur. And these show defects per million tires. And their failure rate, the Decatur tires, is ten times more than any other tire shown on this chart. In Venezuela, they were local tires. In Saudi Arabia, they were the tires that were actually on the right hand side of that chart. So we had no reason to believe at that point that we had a problem. And all the Firestone data that we were shown would indicate very similar trends.

The CHAIRMAN. There is an internal document, which I will give you a copy of, Algizira vehicles. It is to John Thompson who is the Director of Operations and Marketing in Ford Motor Company saying, as you know, "this concern goes back to mid-1997 when we first notified you of this concern. I have to state that I believe the situation to be of key concern which could endanger both the vehicle and more importantly user vehicles. So I am asking what is going on. Do we have a fatality before any action is taken on this subject?" Are you aware of this?

Mr. NASSER. I am aware of it and I am proud of employees like that. Because in the Ford Motor Company, we actually encourage people to come out and talk about issues as they come out. And what we did there is in Saudi Arabia we went ahead and replaced the tires. Because as Firestone mentioned earlier, conditions are different. By the way, when we went to the Goodyear tires in Saudi Arabia, we have not had any problems.

The CHAIRMAN. Well, again, I am glad you are proud of this individual, but he says, I have to say it again, "I am very disappointed that no one has had the decency to send me a letter explaining what is happening." Was he responded to?

Mr. NASSER. I am not aware of the response, but the fact that he felt that it was an environment where he could speak about it and talk about it I think it's something that we should encourage. We went back in Saudi Arabia and we replaced those tires——

The CHAIRMAN. Should you also encourage that he be responded to?

Mr. NASSER. Senator, we replaced all the tires in Saudi Arabia.

The CHAIRMAN. All right. I thank you. I have two more brief questions. There is going to be a witness. And I see you have a chart there that I cannot quite see. It says Explorer's safer than passenger cars. A witness on the next panel is going to make the case that the combination of these tires on an SUV like the Explorer can lead to a fatal rollover. Obviously, you do not agree with that.

Mr. NASSER. We do not. But you can accuse us of being biased and you are probably right. But let us deal with the facts. This is government data based on Department of Transportation. And the data clearly shows that over a 10-year period, and there have been almost four million explorers sold over that period, the Explorer has a better record and serious accidents than the average passenger vehicle and also the average compact sports utility vehicle.

In addition to that, the government data shows that not only is the Explorer safer than the average sports utility vehicle in serious accidents, it is also safer in rollover accidents by a substantial number. Both those percentages, Explorer is safer by almost 30 percent. And this has been true since 1991 when Explorer was introduced.

The CHAIRMAN. Going back to our previous conversation, the recall in Saudi Arabia took place in August 1999, is that right?

Mr. NASSER. That is true.

The CHAIRMAN. And this letter was written in 1997.

Mr. NASSER. Senator, I could take you back in terms of a—letter-by-letter, customer-by-customer. In every single case, we kept going back to Firestone saying is there a problem? Every time we went back, the answer was no defects, customer abuse, unusual conditions. Every time we came back to the U.S. market and asked the same question. Are there any defect trends in the U.S.? Should we be doing something in other markets? And I think you heard earlier the Firestone reaction was we don't have any defects. We should really not go ahead with the replacement program.

The CHAIRMAN. Finally, in his testimony this morning, Secretary Slater urged the conferees of the Transportation appropriations bill to remove provisions that would prohibit the implementation of a consumer rollover rating system until a study is conducted by the National Academy of Sciences. It is my understanding that the study requirement was put into the bill at the behest of the automotive industry. Many believe that the rollover propensity of the Explorer contributes to the severity of these accidents. Would Ford commit to working with NHTSA to implement an appropriate rollover rating system without the further delay of a study by the National Academy of Sciences?

Mr. NASSER. I am not a legislative expert clearly, Senator.

The CHAIRMAN. You have some very high priced help here, sir.

Mr. NASSER. We would support that proposal.

The CHAIRMAN. Thank you. I appreciate that. Senator Bryan.

Senator BRYAN. Thank you very much, Mr. Chairman. Mr. Nasser, you say in your prepared remarks that Ford did not know that there was a defect with the tires until they received confidential claims data from Firestone in July of this year, being 2000. I must say to the layman, this strains Ford's credibility. Because we have had recalls in Saudi Arabia, Malaysia, Thailand, Venezuela, Columbia and Ecuador. And if the testimony of Firestone is correct, they did not agree with those recalls, but those were initiated by Ford. My first question is did Ford initiate those recalls which I have referenced without the concurrence of Firestone?

Mr. NASSER. We did.

Senator BRYAN. You did. So you have got at least a half a dozen countries and maybe more. Give me the benefit of Ford's thinking. I mean, I cannot believe that a company that is as prestigious with all of its history and part of the American automobile icon is saying to Americans that their safety is of less importance than the safety in these other countries. What was Ford's thinking in terms of not initiating a recall much more timely than it did in these other countries?

Mr. NASSER. Senator, when you start to look at the recall actions in Saudi Arabia and in South America, they were very different markets, very different products in the case of Venezuela and Columbia and Ecuador. As you heard from Firestone, they were different tires. And in the case of Saudi Arabia, every time we came back and we asked—and I think it might be appropriate at this point if I can show you some of the data and just indicate to you that every single accident to us is very important. And we react to every single one. So it is not that we knew of a problem and did not react. We just did not know that there were issues here in the U.S.

Senator BRYAN. Let me follow up if I may with that. All right. You say you did not know. Now you do know that there is a problem. And literally millions of people are concerned about the ATX, the ATXII and the Wilderness. And yet, the recall effort has been limited. There are many in the safety advocacy field who say, look. All of those tires have been recalled.

Now, your premise is, look. We did not know. Information was not provided to us. Now we know there is a problem. Would it not be the prudent and responsible sort of thing? Would it not be in the best interest of Ford Motor Company as a responsible corporate citizen to say, look. We are not going to take any chances with the health and safety of our customers. We are going to recall them all and give an opportunity for replacement. What would be wrong with that approach?

Mr. NASSER. That is exactly the right approach. And that is exactly what we are doing. Because if you look at that chart which talks about Firestone tires in the U.S., we are concentrating on those bad tires. There is not much point replacing good tires with good tires. And as Firestone indicated, and the tire industry would tell you, it would actually get in the road of getting bad tires off the vehicles in the industry at this point.

Senator BRYAN. Let me just say, Mr. Nasser, I do not think the public sees it that way. I mean, we are quibbling now with what the engineering data might indicate. There is a concern on the part of the average citizen who does not have the benefit of all of the sophisticated engineering that Ford Motor Company can engage and say, look. I have a serious question as to whether the automobile I am driving, the Ford Explorer, with these tires, is safe. It just strikes to me that in light of what many of us would say would be a very slow response to the situation by both Ford and Firestone that you want to be a proactive and say, look. We are going to replace all of those tires, admittedly establishing a priority for doing so of those categories that you previously outlined.

Mr. NASSER. Senator, I think we spent the whole morning, particularly with Ms. Bailey and Mr. Slater, talking about using facts to manage safety, using technical input to be able to make sure that not only are we making the right decisions, but that we have our priorities set. And if you look at the data there, the tires that are not being recalled are world class tires. You just can't get any better. So I do not really see the point at this point in replacing those good tires with further good tires and taking the tire industry's capability to change over the bad tires.

Senator BRYAN. Let me just ask, because my time is running out. There have been a number of suggestions that would be made to strengthen the role of NHTSA. One of those is to require by law notification whenever a company issues a recall in a foreign country. Would Ford agree or disagree with that?

Mr. NASSER. We would agree with that.

Senator BRYAN. And how about extending the period of record retention which apparently is only 5 years now. There is a sense that that ought to be a longer period of time. Would Ford agree or disagree with that?

Mr. NASSER. Not only do we agree, but we actually continue with record retention way beyond the legislative period.

Senator BRYAN. And increasing the amount of civil penalties which many believe is not adequate, would Ford agree or disagree with that proposal?

Mr. NASSER. We would agree to the extent that it can put more teeth into the legislation and that it actually improves real world safety.

Senator BRYAN. Do you agree that there may be circumstances—and I am not asking you to indicate that the circumstances in this case would be one of those. But that the situation could be so egregious that indeed criminal penalties would be appropriate.

Mr. NASSER. We agree with that.

Senator BRYAN. You agree with that. And to increase the statute of limitations on recalls, would Ford agree or disagree with that?

Mr. NASSER. We agree.

Senator BRYAN. And to amend the rule regarding the statute of limitations on reporting of defects, would Ford agree or disagree with that?

Mr. NASSER. We agree. And we presently abide by a longer statute.

Senator BRYAN. And would you agree or disagree with requiring manufacturers to report lawsuits?

Mr. NASSER. That's part of our proposal. We think that was part of the missing information link that the Federal agency and the automotive manufacturers were not sharing.

Senator BRYAN. And let me say that I complement Ford on that. The final question is that there has been some question about document withholding and all of that sort of thing. My question to you, Mr. Nasser, is Ford prepared to make available to NHTSA, to our Committee, all internal memorandums, documents, letters, any information that relates to this issue without being specifically requested by NHTSA or our Committee to identify the particular document? What I am asking is a full and complete disclosure of all information that the Ford automobile company has that deals with this issue. Are you prepared to make that commitment?

Mr. NASSER. We are. And we have done that. And the last time I looked, we had supplied 100 pages of correspondence and information and technical data.

Senator BRYAN. I thank you for your answer. And I thank you, Mr. Chairman, for letting me go over a couple of minutes.

The CHAIRMAN. Thank you, Senator Bryan. Senator Abraham.

Senator ABRAHAM. Thanks, Mr. Chairman. Mr. Nasser, you commented on the chart here to the left. I was wondering if you would talk a little bit about the other chart that has been put up here?

Senator BRYAN. I think as we have been following this over the last couple of weeks, there has been at least the impression created that your company was inundated with claims and complaints that were unheated. And I am wondering—I am having a little bit of trouble understanding some of the numbers up there and what they refer to. But this seems to address that question. And I am wondering if you might tell us a little bit about the magnitude of these so-called charges, claims, whatever, that you want to lump them together. But the combination, how much had you previously heard from these sources prior to your actions?

Mr. NASSER. We have really been looking at tread separation. I think the whole industry looks at it for many, many years. And interestingly enough, I was reading in the newspaper that we have known about these tread separations for years and years and they have been a problem in the industry. And that there have been lawsuits and so on.

And what I have here on this chart—and it is not even additive—but we added them all together just to get an impact. We added up all the lawsuits, all the property damage claims, all the reports that owners had sent to us, all the dealer reports, all the customer goodwill actions that we had taken. And we put them all together. And we tracked them from 1991 through to the year 2000. And when you add all of those together, you get two reports per year for every million tires in service.

So it is a very, very small number. We review this on a regular basis. We also review the NHTSA data on a regular basis as Mr. Slater and Ms. Bailey indicated this morning, their numbers were equally small. And this is in contrast by the way to the chart on the left hand side. Because the scale—this is defects per million and we were not getting more than two per million in any year. If you go over to the left, the Decatur ATX tires were at 241 defects per million. So you had 240 compared to two. And that's a dramatic difference in terms of the issues.

I would also like to point one other thing out. When you look at the Firestone tires in the U.S., that is a combination of 26 PSI, 32 PSI and interestingly enough, even if you go over to the right hand side there, there are 26 PSI tires that are world class that are not included in this recall. And that is further evidence that it is a tire defect issue.

Senator ABRAHAM. In other words, those numbers there indicate the amount of complaints total all those sources that are listed above per million tires.

Mr. NASSER. Yes.

Senator ABRAHAM. So in the year 1999, it was 1.2 complaints per million. OK. Will you supply the Committee with all of that information? Because I think it is pretty interesting.

Mr. NASSER. We will do that.

Senator ABRAHAM. Second question I had. The question that was just posed to you by Senator Bryant concerned trying to address tires that had not—did not have problems as a matter of broadening your efforts. I was at the truck plant in Wayne, Michigan a couple of weeks ago before the original issues came forward and talked to a lot of people on the line there. I then read just a few days later that that facility had been converted over to help address this issue. And I wondered if you might explain to the committee some of the other actions that are being taken by the company to try to address just the tire problems that we know about as opposed to situations where the tires on vehicles are good and will be replaced by other good tires. What are you doing cumulatively to try to do that in addition to that one facility? And you might just mention that facility because it is obviously one of our significant employers in the State.

Mr. NASSER. We have close down three of our facilities on a temporary basis so we can convert production tires to tires that can be used for replacement tires for our customers to replace bad tires. And that will be 3 weeks and 3 plants.

Our whole attitude, strategy, everything that we are doing in the Ford Motor Company today is aimed at improving the situation for our customers. You do not close plants down lightly, Senator, as you know. And you certainly don't close plants down that have got products lightly. But we did that because we felt it was important that we do everything possible to get as many good tires out in the hands of our customers to replace bad tires. Now, I personally spoke to the CEOs of all of the tire companies so that we could not only encourage them to increase production, but to actually assist them into putting additional molds into production. And that is happening. We feel confident at this point that by the end of November, you probably heard when the recall was first announced that it was going to be spring of next year. We went berserk when we heard that. That was just unacceptable. And the Ford Motor Company, and I must say the tire industry in total including Firestone, have been working together to accelerate that rectification program as quickly as possible.

Senator ABRAHAM. Have the other companies been responsive to these requests?

Mr. NASSER. They have been very responsible.

Senator ABRAHAM. And do you feel that you can obtain an adequate amount to continue to conduct the recall at an acceptable pace?

Mr. NASSER. We have been so far. And I think it will actually improve as we look out over the next 3 or 4 weeks.

Senator ABRAHAM. Well, the Wayne plant manufacturers, the expedition I think along with some other vehicles, what is the impact on the production of those other vehicles then? What do you foresee this year in terms of vehicle production levels as a result of the transfer over to these activities?

Mr. NASSER. Well, we have clearly lost some production, several thousand in each of those plants. But that is not what is our focus at the moment. Our focus is how do we get out our customers more peace of mind with good tires?

Senator ABRAHAM. Thank you. I was actually going to ask some of the questions Senator Bryan did about your response to or consideration of some of the legislation or proposals that we have had before us. But he kind of covered the entire list. So, Mr. Chairman, I notice that my light is on. And I thank you for giving me a chance to ask these questions.

The CHAIRMAN. Thank you, Senator Abraham. I am sorry for the late hour, Mr. Nasser. Thank you for your patience. And we will obviously solicit your input between now and next Wednesday when we propose legislation before the Committee to be marked up. And I thank you for appearing today.

Senator ABRAHAM. Thank you, Mr. Chairman.

[The prepared statement of Mr. Nasser follows:]

PREPARED STATEMENT OF JAC NASSER, PRESIDENT AND CHIEF EXECUTIVE OFFICER, FORD MOTOR COMPANY

Good morning, Chairman McCain and Members of the Committee. I am Jac Nasser, President and CEO of Ford Motor Company. I appreciate the opportunity to be here today to discuss Firestone's tire recall. At Ford, we are very concerned that there are defective tires on some of our vehicles and we will not rest until every bad tire is replaced. I am here today because I know that you and the public have questions about the tire recall, and I want to make sure your questions are answered.

I have been with Ford Motor Company for more than 30 years. I am proud of the great contributions Ford Motor Company has made to improve the standard of living of millions of people around the world. We are deeply committed to our customers, and clearly their safety is uppermost on our minds.

As you know, Firestone manufactured and warranted the recalled tires. However, because so many of these tires were used as original equipment on Ford products, we have taken extraordinary steps to support this recall and ensure the safety of our customers. We are working relentlessly to find and replace bad tires with good tires. That includes making sure that we understand the scope of the problem and finding the root cause. And we continue to be open about any data, statistics or information that we have—and will share any new information as soon as we get it. Ford Motor Company is absolutely committed to doing the right thing to protect our customers and to maintain their trust.

Why This is the Right Action

We believe Firestone's recall is the right action. First, we strongly support Firestone's decision to recall 15" ATX and Decatur-built Wilderness AT tires. Based on the Firestone data we have analyzed, we've determined that these tires are the problem tires. Charts summarizing our detailed analysis of the Firestone data are included in Attachments 1 through 9.

We felt so strongly that this was the right action that we agreed to share the cost of the recall with Firestone—as an incentive for them to do the recall immediately and to allow our dealers to use makes other than Firestone as replacement tires.

What we still don't know is why these tires fail. We are working hard on that.

Tire Issue

This is a tire issue, not a vehicle issue. We have millions of Goodyear tires on 1995 through 1997 Explorers—the same specification tire operating under the same conditions, including 26 psi—and they haven't experienced these problems. Furthermore, non-Decatur made 15" Wilderness tires operate at 26 psi and have not demonstrated tread separation problems.

Ford products—particularly the Explorer—have been highlighted in this recall because most of the recalled tires were used as original equipment *solely* on Ford products. The Explorer was introduced to the public in 1990 with Firestone ATX tires, which stayed in production until mid 1996, when the new Wilderness tire was introduced. During the 1996–1998 model years about 500,000 Explorers were produced with Goodyear tires. The 15" ATX and Wilderness tires were also installed as original equipment on Ford Ranger and F–150. No other vehicle manufacturer used this type of ATX or Wilderness tire as original equipment.

I would like to emphasize that there is nothing unique about the Explorer that is related to tread separations. The documents we provided to NHTSA conclusively show that prior to going into production, the Explorer met exceedingly stringent performance and safety standards.

The Explorer has had an exemplary safety record over the last decade. The most recent data from the Department of Transportation show that the Explorer has a lower fatality rate than both the average passenger car and competitive SUV, as shown in Attachment 10. Additionally, Explorer's fatality rate in rollover accidents is 26 percent lower than other compact SUVs (Attachment 11).

Actions We Have Taken

Now, let's talk about the actions Ford has taken to support the recall and why we believe these are the right actions.

I want to emphasize that Ford did not know there was a defect with the tires until we received the confidential claims data from Firestone in July of this year. It has been standard practice in the automotive industry that tires are the only part of the vehicle not warranted by the vehicle manufacturer. Because tires are separately warranted, they are the only part for which vehicle manufacturers do not receive field performance data.

Looking back, the first signs of trouble came in Saudi Arabia. When reports of tread separation first came to our attention, we asked Firestone to investigate. This included shipping problem tires back to the U.S. for evaluation as well as rigorous high speed testing. They concluded that the tire failures were due to external causes, such as poor repairs, road hazard damage, and extreme operating conditions. But, given the problems our customers were having, we decided to replace the tires with a more puncture resistant tire.

Another market where we experienced tire problems is Venezuela. The situation in Venezuela is complicated by the fact that about three-quarters of the tires were locally produced. Again, Firestone concluded that the tread separations were caused by poor repairs, road hazard damage, and extreme operating conditions. In May of this year, we began replacing all the Firestone tires on Ford Explorers and certain light trucks in Venezuela. As the old tires were returned to us, we examined them and found that 15% of the Venezuelan-made tires had evidence of tread separation.

Concern about the safety of all of our customers, including our U.S. customers, drove us to look aggressively for evidence of a defect in the U.S. at the same time we were taking actions overseas. As early as April of 1999, we were searching all available databases—our own and the government's. We asked Firestone to check its records. And we had new tires tested under three separate, severe test conditions to try to cause tread separation to happen. Last Fall, we kicked off a tire inspection test program in Texas, Arizona and Nevada. No defect trend was found.

Because there have been a number of questions regarding our investigation of data on tread separations, I would like to explain the data available to Ford and our review of these data. We receive data which track quality issues from owners, dealers and our warranty claims. These data are monitored regularly. We also watch property damage claims, personal injury claims, and lawsuits filed against Ford. In conjunction with our investigation of overseas issues, we reviewed all of these data sources and found no trend of tread separation issues on Firestone tires in the U.S.

We also looked at two government databases. NHTSA's Vehicle Owner Questionnaire (VOQ) reports track consumer complaints filed with NHTSA. Also, the Department of Transportation maintains data on vehicle fatalities (FARS). Again, neither of these government sources revealed an obvious defect trend.

It is important to clarify that there are several types of performance data maintained by *tire* manufacturers that are not regularly available to auto companies. First, tire manufacturers keep adjustment data, similar to what we call warranty data in the auto industry. Adjustments may cover issues ranging from manufacturing defects to abnormal wear or tire appearance issues. Tire makers also keep claims data, which represent customer requests for payment resulting from property damage or personal injury. Finally, tire companies also keep track of lawsuits filed against them claiming injury related to tire defects. None of these data sources are available to automakers on a regular basis.

Because the tires are warranted by Firestone, much of the quality and performance data is included in Firestone's internal databases, but not Ford's. Additionally, property damage, personal injury and legal claims would most often be filed with the tire maker, not the auto manufacturer. For example, while there were over 2,700 claims included in Firestone's data, a review of Ford's records show that as of May 10, 2000, approximately 50 claims had been filed with Ford.

When NHTSA opened their investigation, and required Firestone to assemble and provide data on property damage, personal injury, and lawsuits, Ford insisted on obtaining that data as well. When we received the data late in July, we quickly analyzed it and identified the problem tires that were recalled August 9.

Customer Focus

As I said, our top priority is to replace faulty tires as fast as possible. As of September 7, about 1.8 million tires have been replaced—about 28 percent of the total population of affected tires. We worked with the tire industry to increase production of 15-inch tires which will increase supply by more than 250,000 tires per month by the end of September. We suspended production at three assembly plants for two weeks beginning at the end of August, adding approximately 70,000 tires to the replacement population. On Friday of last week, I extended the suspension for another week. We have engaged over 3,200 Ford and Lincoln-Mercury dealers to perform tire replacements.

We've also made a major effort to communicate information about the Firestone recall to our customers. For example, we have opened an additional call center to deal specifically with inquiries on the tire recall. We are using our website to provide detailed information on the recall action. And we are running national and local newspaper and television ads to alert customers to the recall and show them how to tell if their vehicles are affected.

Our support of this recall extends to our full cooperation with NHTSA. We have provided extensive disclosure to NHTSA in regards to this action. Our policy is to be as open as possible, sharing what we know, when we know it.

Conclusion

Last week I made a commitment to work with the industry to implement an "early warning system" to detect the first signs of tire defects on vehicles already on the road. This system must utilize comprehensive real world data that—we now know—is so critical to spotting defect patterns. I also committed that Ford will advise U.S. safety authorities of safety actions taken in overseas markets and vice-versa.

This has been a difficult situation. Our first priority is to replace bad tires with good tires as quickly as possible. The safety, trust and peace of mind of our consumers are paramount to Ford Motor Company.

Testimony of Ford Motor Company

Index of Attachments to Written Testimony

1. Tread Separation Claims Rate for Firestone 15-inch and 16-inch
2. Claims Data—Claims for Firestone Tires by Tire Size
3. Claims Data—Claims for Firestone P235/75R15 ATX and Wilderness Tires by Type of Claim
4. Claims Data—Tread Separation Claims for Firestone Tires by Tire Size
5. Claims Data—Tread Separation Claims Rate for Firestone P235/75R15 ATX and Wilderness Tires for 1996 Tire Production Year
6. Claims Data—Tread Separation Claims Rate for Firestone P235/75R15 Wilderness Tires by Tire Production Year and Plant
7. Claims Data—Tread Separation Claims Rate for Firestone P235/75R15 ATX by Time in Service at Claim, Tire Production Year, and Plant
8. Claims Data—Tread Separation Claims Rate for Firestone P235/75R15 Wilderness by Time in Service at Claim, Tire Production Year, and Plant (Scale 0 to 700)
9. Claims Data—Tread Separation Claims Rate for Firestone P235/75R15 Wilderness by Time in Service at Claim, Tire Production Year, and Plant (Scale 0 to 70)

10. Fatality Rate Comparison—Explorer Compared to Passenger Cars and Compact SUVs
11. Fatality Rate Comparison—Explorer Compared to Other SUVs—All Accident Types and Rollover Accidents

Attachment 1

Tread Separation Claims Rate for Firestone 15-inch and 16-inch Tires

Production Years 1995-1999 and Claims Years 1995-1999

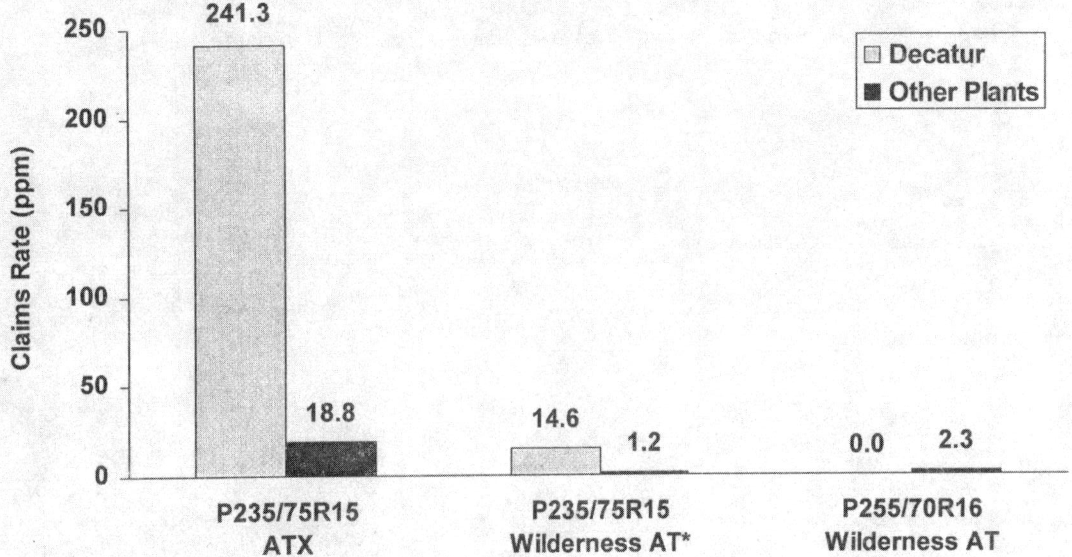

* P235/75R15 Wilderness AT 15-inch production began in 1996

Ford Motor Company

Attachment 2

Claims for Firestone Tires by Tire Size

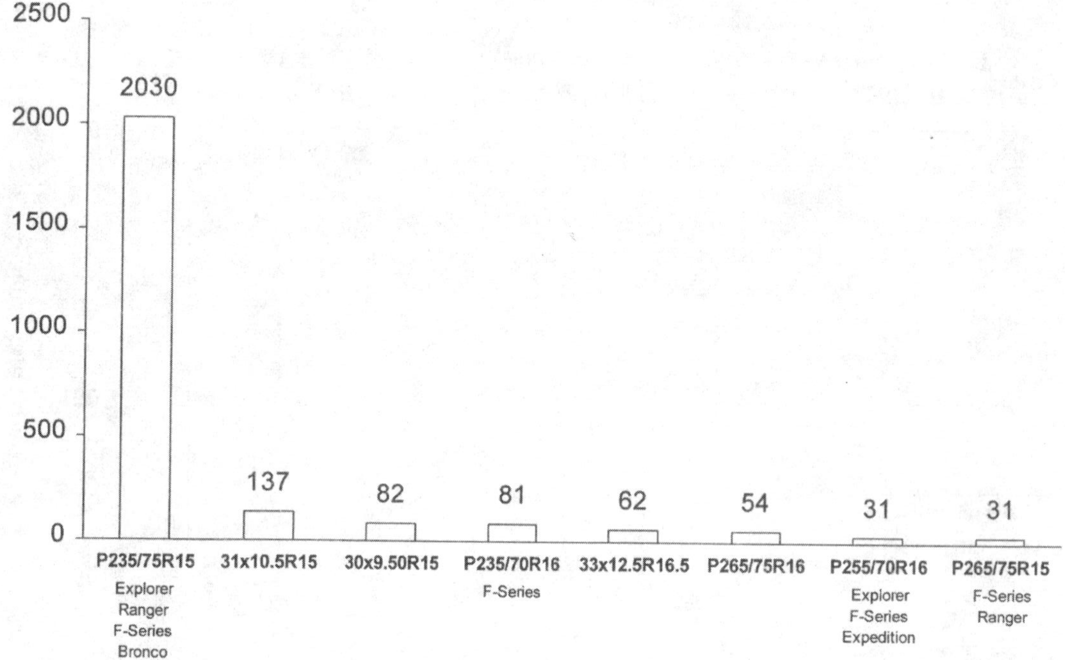

Firestone Property Damage and Injury Claims and Lawsuits Submitted Pursuant to NHTSA Inquiry
Tire Sizes with More Than 30 Claims
Tires with Ford Original Equipment Application Noted

Ford Motor Company

Attachment 3

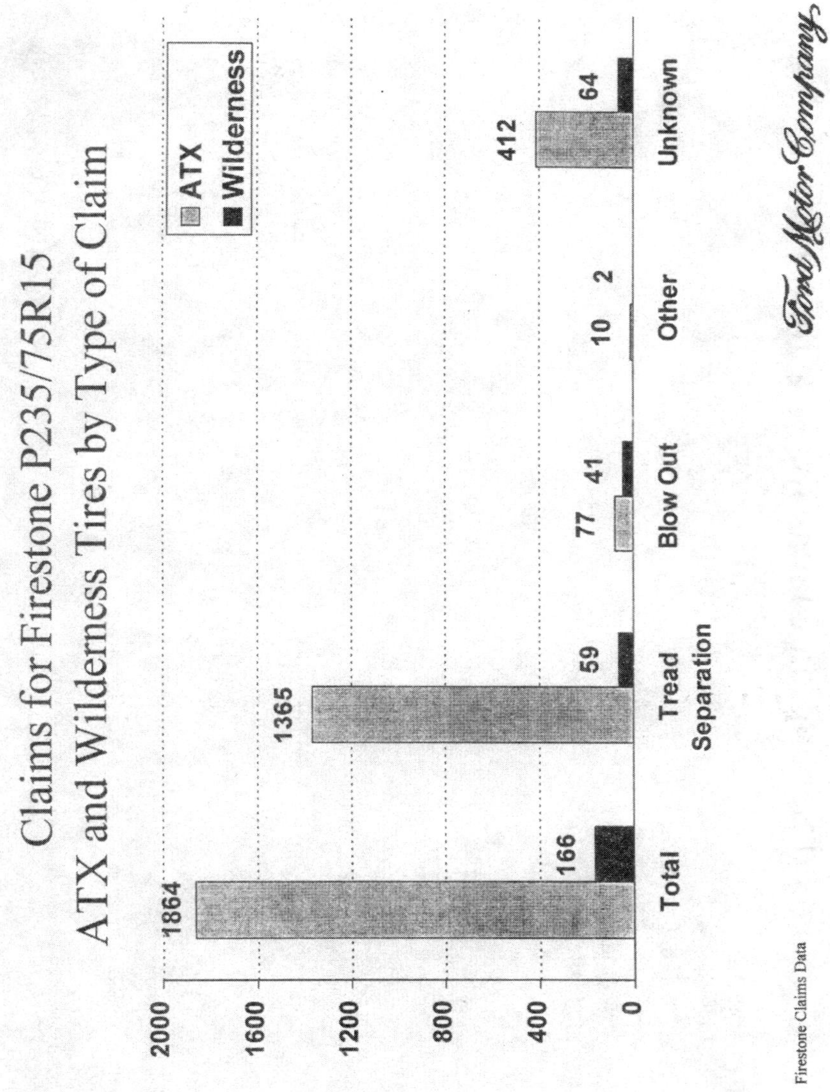

Attachment 4

Tread Separation Claims for Firestone Tires by Tire Size

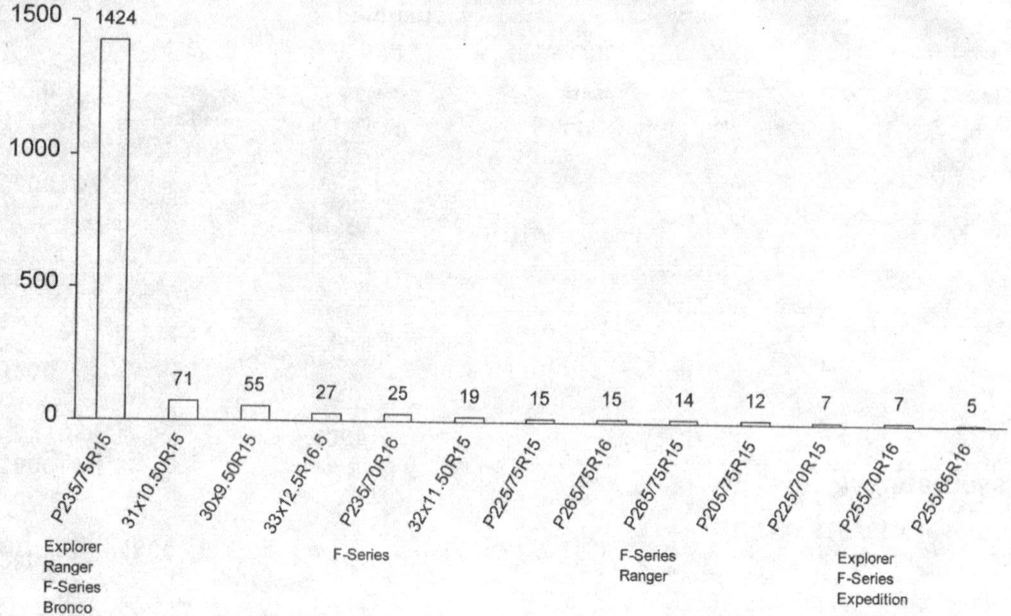

Firestone Claims Data
Tire Sizes with at least 5 Tread Separation Claims
Tires with Ford Original Equipment Application Noted

Ford Motor Company

Attachment 5

Tread Separation Claims Rate for Firestone P235/75R15 ATX and Wilderness Tires for 1996 Tire Production Year

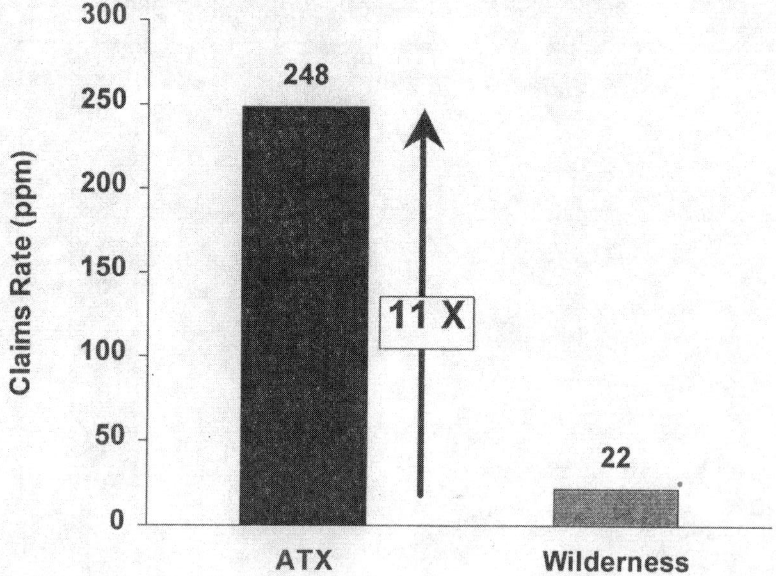

Firestone Claims and Production Data

Ford Motor Company

Attachment 6

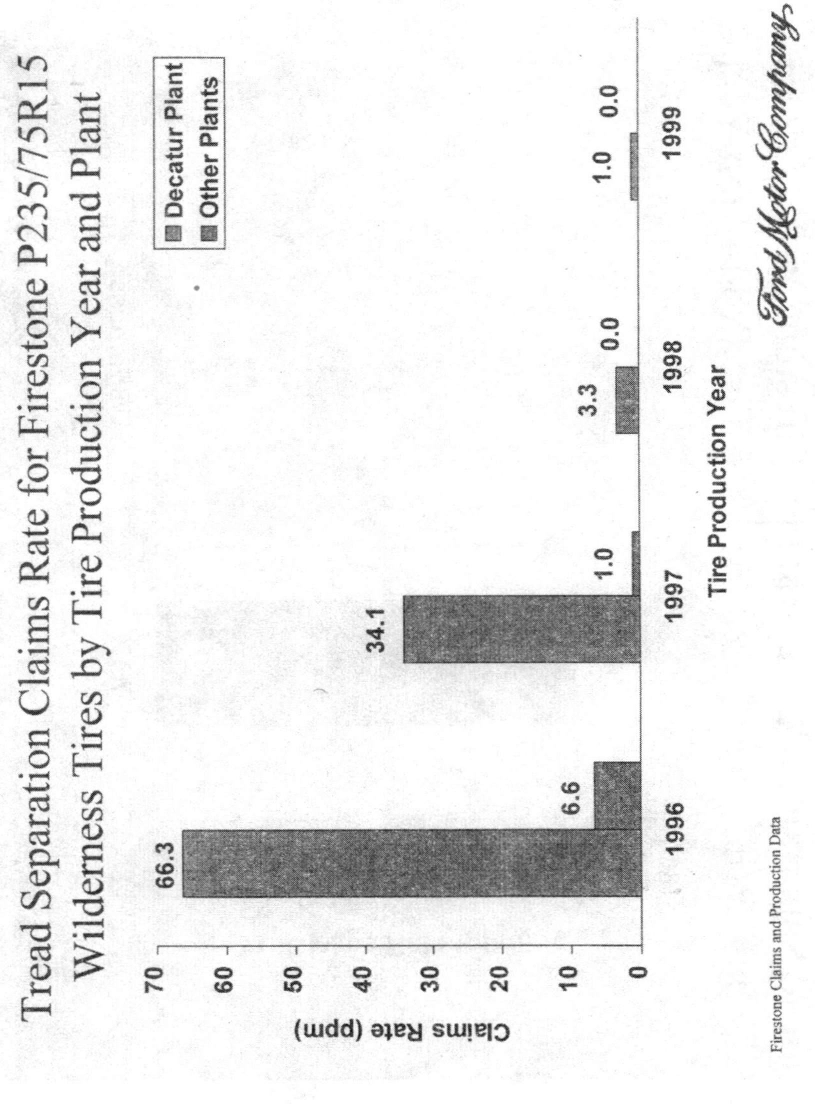

Attachment 7

Tread Separation Claims Rate for Firestone P235/75R15 ATX

by Time in Service at Claim, Tire Production Year, and Plant

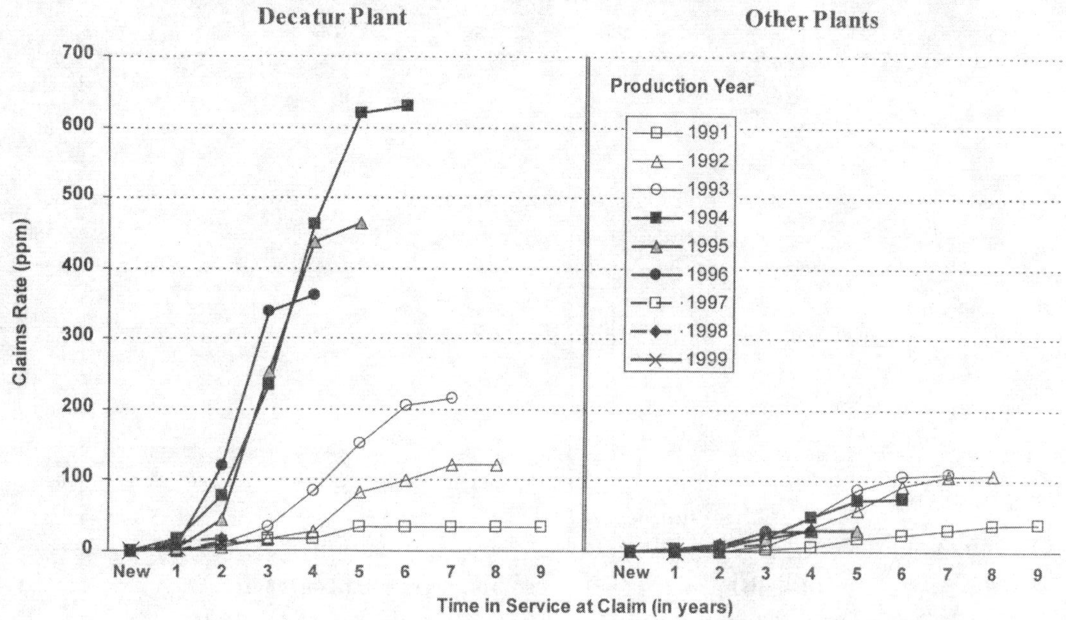

Firestone Claims and Production Data

Ford Motor Company

Attachment 8

Tread Separation Claims Rate for Firestone P235/75R15 Wilderness

by Time in Service at Claim, Tire Production Year, and Plant

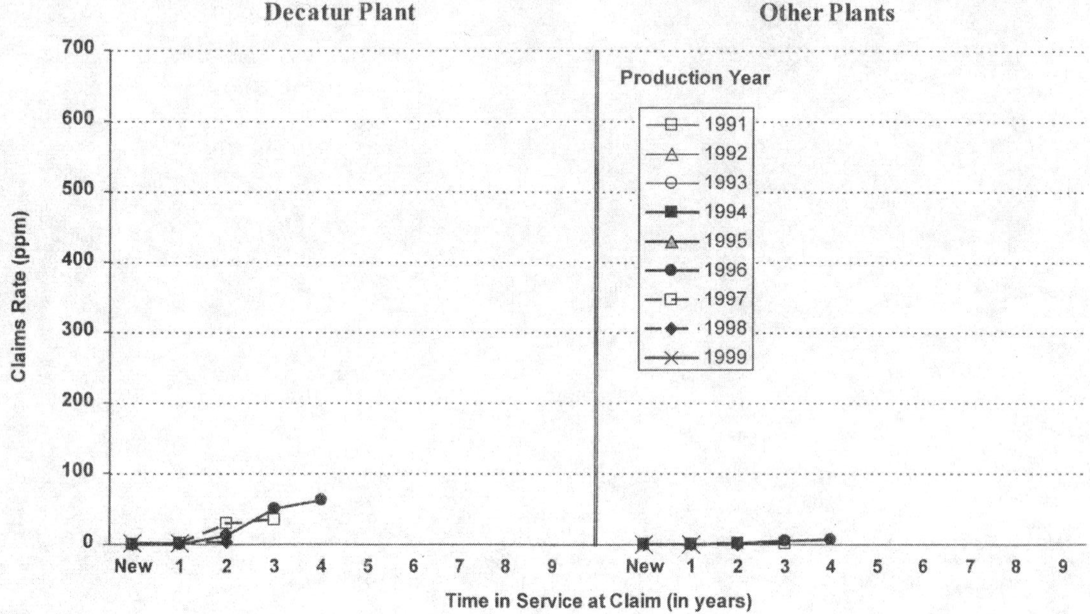

Firestone Claims and Production Data

Ford Motor Company

Attachment 9

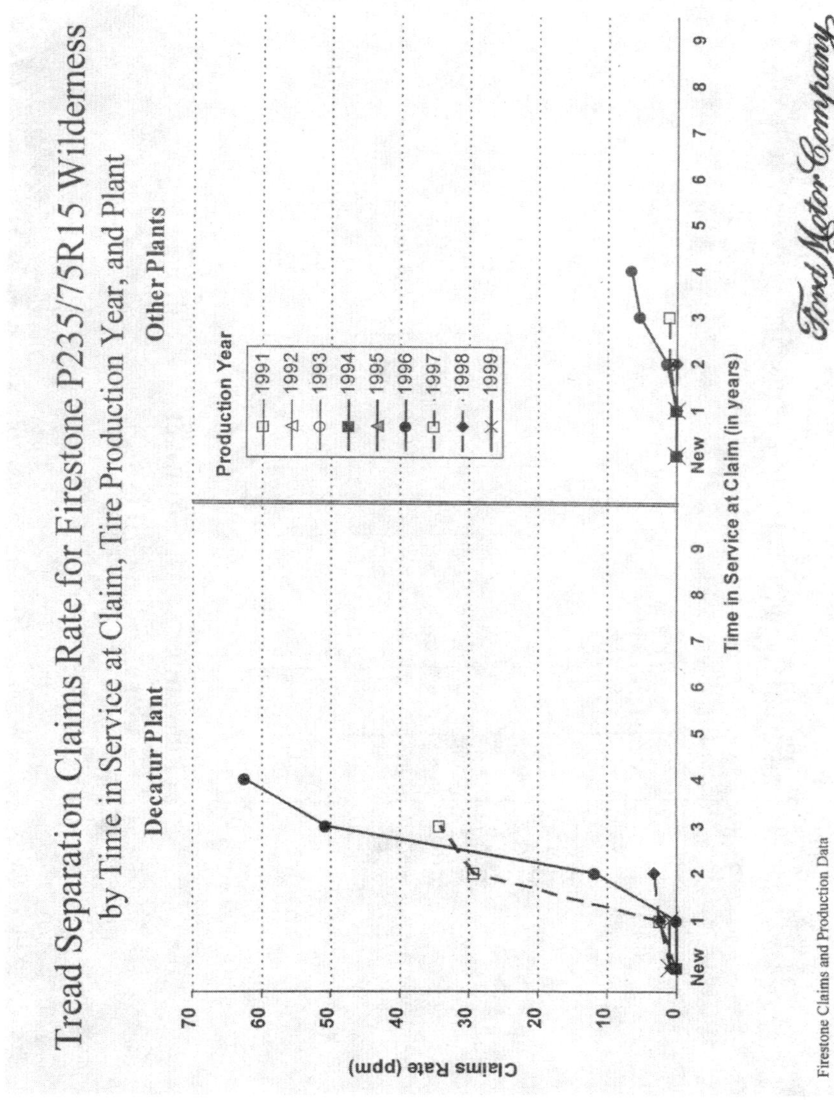

Attachment 10

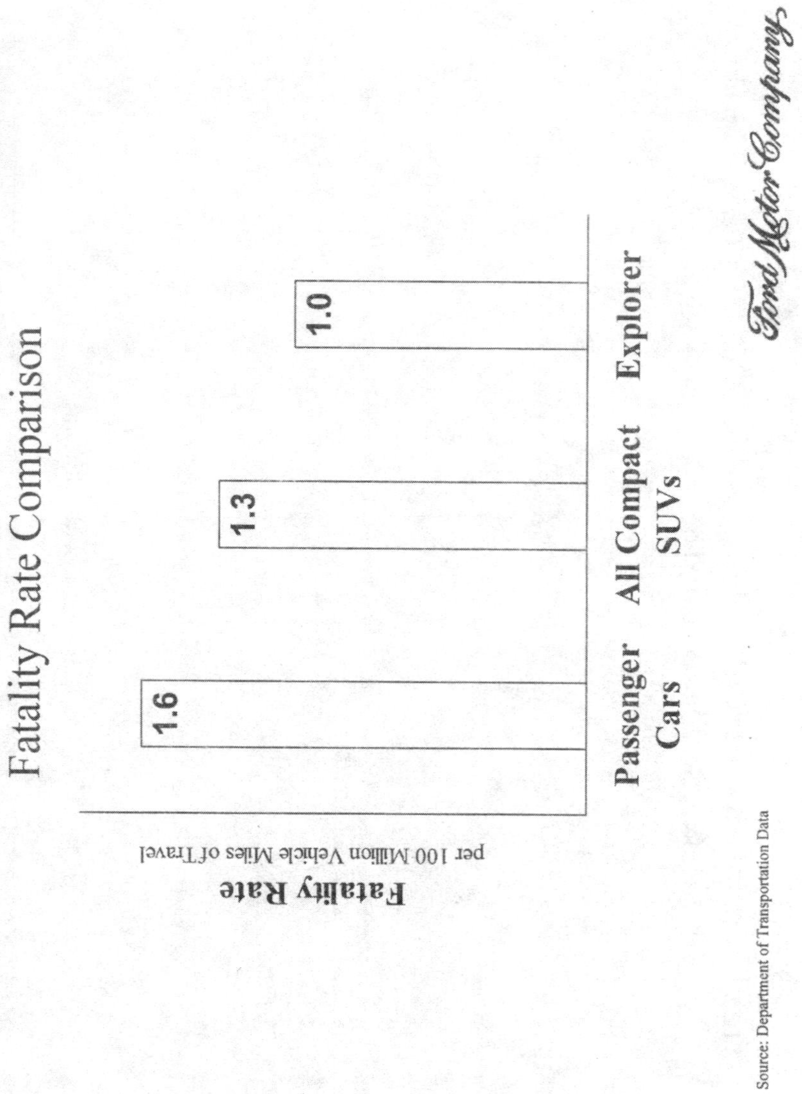

Attachment 11

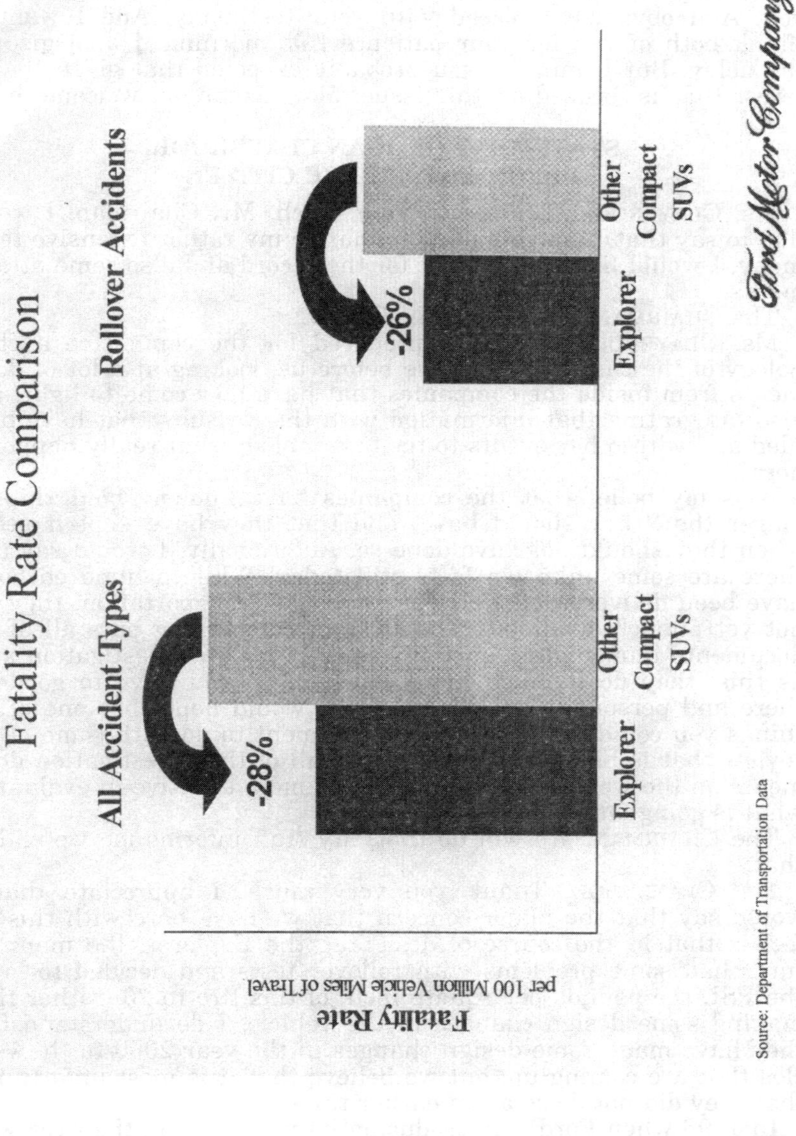

The CHAIRMAN. Thank you very much. Finally, we will hear from Ms. Joan Claybrook, who is the President of Public Citizen, and Mr. Clarence Ditlow, who is the Executive Director of the Center for Auto Safety. It is nice to see you again, Ms. Claybrook. Thank you. And obviously proceed with your testimony. And I want to thank both of you for your patience this morning. I apologize for the delay. But I am sure you probably expected that given the interest that is focused on this issue. Ms. Claybrook, welcome back.

STATEMENT OF JOAN CLAYBROOK, PRESIDENT, PUBLIC CITIZEN

Ms. CLAYBROOK. Thank you very much, Mr. Chairman. I would like to say that I am going to summarize my rather extensive testimony. I would like to submit it for the record and also some attachments.

The CHAIRMAN. Yours too, Mr. Ditlow.

Ms. CLAYBROOK. We have prepared for the committee a chronology of the case that we have before us, looking at a lot of documents from inside the companies that have now come to light, and also integrating that information with the lawsuits that have been filed and with other events to try to establish what really happened here.

It is my belief that the companies have known about this for longer than they should have, and that they have kept it secret when they should not have done so. Additionally, I would say that there are some unknown facts still today. While a hundred boxes have been delivered to the Department of Transportation, they are not yet publicly available. The DOT in rulemaking puts all of the documents immediately on the web. But for an investigation such as this, they do it much more slowly. And you have to go down there and personally get documents. I would hope that one of the things you could encourage the department to do with some of the review that is now going on is to put all of the investigation documents on the web so that we can all be more effective in evaluating what is going on.

The CHAIRMAN. We will do that. My staff informs me we will do that.

Ms. CLAYBROOK. Thank you very much. I appreciate that. I would say that the major concern that we have here with this defect is that in the course of designing the Explorer, the manufacturer had some problems with rollover tests and decided to lower the PSI, the pounds per square inch, of this tire to 26, rather than making some design changes in the vehicle. I do understand that they have made some design changes in the year 2000 to the vehicles that are coming up, but we believe that it is most unfortunate that they did not do so at an earlier time.

In 1996 when Ford was producing its vehicles and the tires were being produced in Venezuela, I just wanted to make sure that the Committee was aware that Ford instructed that the tires in Venezuela be upgraded from the U.S. tires and that a nylon ply be added to the tires manufactured in Venezuela. And also, there was a stiffer shock absorber and some reinforcement added to the suspension.

I agree with the lawyers inside Firestone and Ford that they did have an obligation under current law to notify the Department of Transportation of foreign recalls. There is a provision in the statute that says they have to supply DOT all notices to dealers. But there's sort of an overarching, extra territoriality provision in U.S. law that says that U.S. law cannot govern foreign operations. But this was a U.S. manufacturer with a U.S. made product notifying dealers abroad of concerns about what they were selling in the United States.

There are a number of documents also that have come to light, some of which you have highlighted which show that there was quite a bit of data available to these companies along the way. I compare this recall to the Firestone 500—and I brought a picture of it. This was an investigation of 20 years ago. It looked similar to what is happening today. There are many other similarities, including a coverup by the company then. When everything was said and done, those top officials were all removed from the company. And we thought it was a new day at Firestone. But apparently it was not.

Also, the company accused owners of not properly inflating their tires or of abusing their tires then as they have today. Except for in testimony this morning when they discounted that.

To me the most important thing to come out of all of this, this tragedy for the American public, is new legislation. And I commend the Chair and his efforts in announcing the markup next week. We are very enthusiastic about this. We will do anything that we can to help the committee to raise that maximum penalty, now $925,000, which is a joke. And we would urge that there be criminal penalties included here as there are for the Food and Drug Administration, the Environmental Protection Agency, and the Consumer Product Safety Commission. NHTSA is one of the few agencies that does not have authority to bring criminal penalties.

Also, we support the extension of time for the retention of documents, statute of limitations and for self-certification. Right now, Mr. Chairman, if a company certifies its product to meet NHTSA standards, it need not test it ahead of time. Such testing should be a mandatory requirement.

I took a brief look at the proposal by the Secretary which they are sending up to Congress today. And I certainly endorse the additional authorities that he has proposed.

I would like to say one thing about the budget. I think we ought to look at it this way, just as an example for someone such as yourself who is so knowledgeable about the Defense Department: We spend billions of dollars on defense, but more members of the military are killed in motor vehicle crashes than are killed during military duty. And that seems to drive the point home to me.

I do believe that there are——

The CHAIRMAN. I think you make a good point. My point was that every year at the end of the year, and we are about to reach that point again, where in a smoke filled room somewhere, there's billions—billions—maybe tens of billions—added in all kinds of pork barrel projects, all kinds of obscene and outrageous things. At least you would think that with those tens of billions perhaps, maybe a few million could have been added to NHTSA's budget in their zeal to increase all of the spending. See my point? That was my point.

Ms. CLAYBROOK. Oh, I know. I know your point. And I completely agree with it. But the problem for NHTSA is that it is a regulatory agency. It is Uncle Sam, not Uncle Sugar. There are two different entities up here unfortunately.

The third point I would make is that we believe that there should be consideration of an expanded recall. But all of the data is not yet on the public record, and I will not go into all of the particulars. I brought two tires here today. One is the 15 inch and one is the 16 inch. The 16 inch is not being recalled. The 15 inch is. You can see that they have a very similar pattern of failure. One of the patterns is that these tires do not fail in the early years of production, but in the later years after they are on the road for some time, the 16 inch Wilderness, this one, was not manufactured—the Wilderness tire was not manufactured and on the road until 1996.

And since data is usually a year or 2 years behind an evaluation, we do not yet have all the data on the Wilderness tire. We certainly do not have the most current information. The evaluation by Ford Motor Company of the Firestone data, claims data, to define this recall was current as of the 1st of May only. That brings me to a point that I emphasize and that is the system of data and evaluation and the process that sparks a recall inside of NHTSA.

Any statistical analysis is flawed if the data set that you are using is flawed. Unfortunately, if you base conclusions on claims or from consumer complaints, you must be aware they are a small portion of what is actually happening out there on the road. And to measure it from the tires as they did at DOT, 90 claims or 46 claims or complaints against the 40 million tires that were manufactured is totally irrelevant. You have to look at factors like: are there deaths? Are there injuries? Is there a catastrophic problem? In this case, the accidents were a catastrophic type of event where people were doing what they are supposed to do and then find themselves terribly injured or their familiy members dead.

One of the things that is missing right now on the record is information about what tests Firestone did and what tests Ford did of the 26 PSI-inflated tire. I do not think that that data is publicly available yet. I do not think that it is available to your Committee. I would suggest that it be subpoenaed if you do not get it. You have asked them to give it to you voluntarily. This data should be submitted because, under current law, companies do not have to test the exact tire or product before they certify it.

I do not believe, as it was revealed in the House side, that Ford ever did tests at 26 PSI, which is a very low PSI for this vehicle. I do not know about Firestone. But I think that you ought to demand that they submit that information to your committee immediately. Without it, we do not really know the extent to which these tires were first tested or what the tests showed. That information would greatly help to define this recall.

The CHAIRMAN. We will ask for it.

Ms. CLAYBROOK. Thank you. We have been through the discussion of NHTSA. So I will not raise that issue other than as a concern about the way that they evaluate statistical data. I certainly endorse your call to have an Inspector General investigation of this. I would ask that the IG look in particular at this whole issue of statistical evaluation, because sometimes when NHTSA is doing investigations of defects, they close their investigation because they cannot find a statistical correlation. An example is a door lock case I had suggested that they look at. And they closed the investigation. But you cannot find statistics on whether a door lock does not work in the statistical data base where the doors pop open but do not stay broken after an accident.

Finally, I would ask that in your legislation, Mr. Chairman, that you consider giving NHTSA the charge of issuing an upgraded tire standard by a certain date, an upgraded roof crush standard by a certain date. I do not know whether you are aware, but the roof crush standard is also 32 years old. And when you look at the rollovers, look what happens to the roof. That should not happen to a roof in a rollover. And what the standard says is that on a static basis, you put onto a car, one and a half times its unloaded weight and that is the standard for rollover. It is ridiculous that it is not a dynamic standard.

Furthermore, the tire quality grading standard applies only to car tires, not to SUV and truck tires. Also, there needs to be a rollover prevention standard. Right now, the arguments in the appropriations committee are over consumer information requirements. But there also needs to be a minimum standard, at least for SUVs that have a propensity to roll over.

I had to laugh as I listened to the testimony about the tire inflation indicator device because I proposed this in 1978 after the first Firestone recall. All of the industry then opposed this measure to tell the consumer when there is low tire inflation, and to put it on the dashboard.

I have several other minor proposals for inclusion in the legislation. We appreciate very much the work you are doing, your willingness to move very quickly. I do not think that this Congress should go home and ask people to vote for them until they fix this problem and can assure their consumers and constituents that this will not happen again. Thank you, very much.

[The prepared statement of Ms. Claybrook follows:]

PREPARED STATEMENT OF JOAN CLAYBROOK, PRESIDENT, PUBLIC CITIZEN

Mr. Chairman and Members of the Committee:

I am pleased to accept your invitation to testify today on the Firestone tire defect that has killed at least 88 and injured 250 people, most of them in Ford Explorers. I am President of Public Citizen, a national public interest organization founded by Ralph Nader in 1971 with 150,000 members nationwide. I served as Administrator of the National Highway Traffic Safety Administration in the U.S. Department of Transportation from 1977 to 1981. This agency is responsible for administering the recall of the Firestone tires. The Firestone 500 recall occurred in 1978 when I was Administrator.

Much has been written and broadcast in the past month about the lethal combination of Ford Explorers and Firestone tires. This is a design defect exacerbated by the fact that Ford required a low inflation pressure of 26 psi to mitigate rollover problems with these vehicles. Firestone ATX, ATX II and Wilderness tires on Ford Explorers are overheating with highway use, causing the tread to separate and the SUVs to experience catastrophic crashes, not infrequently rolling over and causing fatal injuries. At least 135 people world-wide have died. This tragedy is teaching the public as well as policy makers a number of lessons. I would like to comment on five issues and make recommendations for more effective enforcement of the nation's motor vehicle safety defect laws.

1. Ford and Firestone covered up safety problems with the tire/SUV combination for a decade. Coverups will continue without corrective action by NHTSA.

The Ford Explorer was first offered for sale in March 1990. Numerous Ford internal documents show the company engineers recommended changes to the vehicle design after it rolled over in company tests prior to introduction, but other than a few minor changes, the suspension and track width were not changed because this would have delayed the introduction date by as much as ten months. Instead, Ford, which sets the specifications for the manufacture of its tires, decided to remove air from the tires, lowering the recommended psi to 26. It appears Ford never fully tested the tires at this level. The Firestone-recommended psi molded into the tire for maximum load is 35 psi.

Within a year of introduction, lawsuits against Ford and Firestone were filed for tire failures that resulted in crashes and rollovers. At least five cases were filed by 1993, and many others followed in the early 1990s. Almost all were settled, and settled with gag orders prohibiting the attorneys and the families from disclosing information about the cases or their documentation to the public or DOT. When lawsuits are filed against a company about a safety defect, the company organizes an internal investigation to assemble information and analysis about the allegations. Top company officials are kept informed about all lawsuits against the company, particularly when they accumulate concerning one problem. There is no question the companies knew they had a problem. But they kept it secret.

During the early 1990s, Ford was concerned with improving the rolling resistance of the tires to be used on the 1995 model Explorer, apparently because of the reduced fuel economy with the low 26 psi inflation level. Changes were made to the 1995 model's suspension system, but these did not lower the center of gravity, an essential element in rollover susceptibility.

In 1996, several state agencies in Arizona began having major problems with tread separations on Firestone tires on Explorers. According to news reports, various agencies demanded new tires, and Firestone sent six engineers to Arizona to conduct an investigation of the complaints, tested the tires and asserted that the tires had been abused or under-inflated.

By the end of 1996, at least 15 lawsuits had been filed.

The Ford Explorer and its sister vehicles with Firestone tires were sold across the globe. In 1998, Ford and Firestone exchanged correspondence and had discussions about tire failures in Middle Eastern, Asian and South American countries. Tires were tested and analyzed. Dealers complained bitterly to Ford and Firestone from 1997 to 2000 about deaths and injuries in Ford Explorers, the adverse effect these were having on sales and delays in getting any relief.

In January 1998, Glenn Drake, Ford's regional marketing manager in the United Arab Emirates e-mails other Ford officials: "If this was a single case, I would accept Firestone's response as they are the experts in the tire business, case closed. However, we now have three cases and it is possible that Firestone is not telling us the whole story to protect them from a recall or a lawsuit."

In 1996, Ford instructed Firestone to upgrade the tires in Venezuela by adding a nylon ply to the tires it manufactured there for additional strength, and Ford made suspension changes to the Explorer, adding a stiffer shock absorber and reinforcement of the suspension. But Ford did not specify adding the nylon ply for U.S.-made Firestone tires nor did it change the U.S. made Explorer suspension at this time.

Ford eventually decided to conduct its own recall without Firestone and replace the tires in the various foreign countries in 1999 and 2000 (called a "customer notification enhancement action"). Ford did this without Firestone because the tire company was fearful a recall would require notification of NHTSA. A March 1999 Ford memo reveals "Firestone legal has some major reservations about the plan to notify customers and offer them an option . . . They feel that the U.S. D.O.T. will have to be notified of the program, since the product is sold in the U.S."

In May 2000, a top Ford official in Venezuela was quoted in the press as saying the company was replacing the tires there because in Venezuela "the highways allow drivers to travel at high speeds for a sustained period of time, leading to the loosening of the rolling surface of the tire, its consequent blowout and the accident."

On August 30, 2000, the Venezuelan safety regulatory agency, Indecu, concluded after an investigation that Firestone and Ford "met to plan ways out of a situation that was affecting their commercial interests, at the price of causing damage, destruction and death," and announced it is recommending possible criminal enforcement for involuntary manslaughter. Neither Ford nor Firestone informed the National Highway Traffic Safety Administration of this recall, euphemistically labeled a "No Charge Service Program Award Notification."

Recently numerous Firestone documents have become available revealing the company had reason to know since 1997 from property damage and injury claims and tire performance data such as warranty adjustments and financial analysis of such claims that its tires were failing. Several documents show a large jump in claims involving tread separations in 1997 and 1998. During all these years the company disclaimed any problem—to consumers, to state government officials and to Ford. One company chart reveals that tread separations for the Wilderness tire increased 194 percent in 1999 from 1998. Test data on the tires by Ford and Firestone are still not available.

By the end of 1999, four months before NHTSA opened its investigation, at least 59 lawsuits had been filed. A total of at least 35 deaths and 130 injuries were involved in the lawsuits or notice of lawsuits to the companies by May, 2000.

Incidentally, there are a number of parallels between this recall in 2000 and the 1978 recall of the Firestone 500. Most particularly, there was a documented coverup by Firestone of the 500 defect, spurred by the lack of a Firestone replacement tire. When the coverup was disclosed, the top management of the company was replaced. Firestone was severely damaged financially and in reputation. But a key difference is that the Firestone 500 was used on passenger cars, which rarely rolled over with tire failure. NHTSA documented 41 deaths with the Firestone 500 case, which involved about seven million tires recalled.

Once again, when confronted with accusations about the performance of the tire, Firestone has misleadingly claimed owner abuse (i.e. under-inflation, rough use or improper fix). Neither Ford nor Firestone designed a margin of safety into its vehicles and tires.

2. The National Highway Traffic Safety Administration needs additional legislative authority to assure that manufacturers obey the law, report safety defects and recall unsafe products.

To prevent coverups of safety defects in the future, the National Traffic and Motor Vehicle Safety Act should be amended. In March 2000 the agency sent legislation to the Congress which would make some improvements, but additional authority is needed. The Congress should:

a. Increase civil penalties for failure to recall a defective vehicle or part or withholding information from the agency. Now the maximum penalty is $925,000, hardly a deterrent for multinational corporations. The penalty for each violation should be increased from $1,000 to $10,000 (as at the Environmental Protection Agency); the violation for withholding documents should be per day rather than per document as it is now (no matter how long it is withheld). There should be no maximum penalty.

b. As in the Food and Drug Administration and the Environmental Protection Agency laws, there should be criminal penalties for reckless endangerment and knowing and willful refusal to recall a defective vehicle or part or for withholding information that results in deaths and injuries. Chairman John Moss, after reviewing the Firestone 500 debacle in 1978, recommended criminal penalties be added to the NHTSA statute.

c. As recommended by NHTSA's proposed bill, a company should be required by law to test its products before self-certifying for compliance with the agency's standards. Such testing is not now required by law.

d. The statute of limitations for NHTSA to mandate a recall is now eight years for vehicles and three years for tires from the date of manufacture. It should be extended, as the agency recommends, to 10 years for vehicles and five years for tires. The statute should be tolled, however, when companies conceal defects. The agency should have authority to require a company to purchase replacement parts from a competitor if necessary where there is an imminent hazard and be able to require reimbursement to consumers who made repairs or bought replacements prior to the recall.

e. There is disagreement about whether the current law requiring manufacturers to send NHTSA copies of all notices sent to dealers and owners about a defect is applicable in this case. Ford sent notices to foreign dealers about a defect in a product made and sold in the U.S. and also sold abroad. Does the fact that the notice was sent to foreign dealers negate Ford's responsibility to notify NHTSA? I don't think so, but certainly the law should be clarified that this is a company's responsibility in this age of globalization. Companies should also have a duty to give NHTSA early warnings based on fatality, injury, warranty or other data it gathers, and the agency should be able to get relevant information from insurers.

f. NHTSA's budget needs to be larger, much larger, particularly for enforcement. Ninety-four percent of transportation deaths occur on the highway, yet NHTSA has only a tiny percentage of the transportation budget. Although it has been increased in recent years, and I thank the Appropriations Committees for that, it is still 30 percent below, in real dollars, what it was when I left the agency at the beginning of 1981. Its enforcement budget is about one-half of the 1980 budget. It has fewer than 20 engineer/investigators working on vehicle safety defects for the entire country. The Congress should add at least $20 million to the agency's 2001 budget for additional staff and capacity. Look at it this way: We spend hundreds of billions of dollars for defense, but more members of the military are killed and injured in motor vehicle crashes than in military duty. The members of the 106th Congress should not be able to go home for election and tell the voters they have acted to prevent another future catastrophe without sending legislation to the President for signature.

3. The Firestone/Ford recall should be expanded to cover all ATX, ATX II and Wilderness tires to protect the public from this catastrophic defect, and all data and information should be made public to restore public trust.

Much of the data on which Ford based its analysis of Firestone claims data is still not public or subject to outside scrutiny (such as how many tires were made at each plant and when—an important factor since the defect appears to emerge after two to four years of use), and it is based on information only through April 2000. None of the recent information that has been pouring into the companies and NHTSA as the public is getting informed about the problem is included. It also covers only claims data—claims for compensation for injury or property damage. It does not cover warranty claims or adjustment data for tire failures. It does not cover any information known to Ford (although there will be duplication between Ford and Firestone data) such as tire test data, including at 26 psi. It also does not cover new information now known by NHTSA about claims.

On September 1, after analyzing recent data (complaints, lawsuits, injuries, including information submitted to date from Ford and Firestone), NHTSA determined that the recall should be enlarged to cover another 1.4 million tires. NHTSA said it is still investigating to determine if the recall should be enlarged further. It issued a consumer advisory because Firestone refused to enlarge the recall, an indication of Firestone's attitude toward a safety defect that gives the consumer no warning and can result in death and severe injury when the vehicle is operated normally. This same attitude was evident in Firestone's offer made on August 16 in public newspaper ads that it would reimburse owners who bought other tires, but the offer also ended on August 16! Had it not been for a temporary restraining order issued by a federal judge in Louisville preventing the company from discontinuing the one-day offer, Firestone might have faced a massive consumer revolt, picket lines, more consumer lawsuits and more disputes with its largest customer, Ford Motor Company, which is pressing to get the tires replaced quickly with tires from other manufacturers as well as Firestone.

There is every indication that this problem is a design defect that affects all the tires produced. In the Firestone 500 case, the company at first asserted that only 400,000 tires were defective, those produced in the Decatur plant. But during NHTSA's investigation, as more data were available and company documents were secured and analyzed, we found that the tread separation on the 500 was a design performance defect. The company knew about it for at least three years and never informed NHTSA, and it was at the same time making running changes on the production line to correct the problem in new tires.

There are other indications that the companies should expand the recall. An analysis released September 1 of about 90 filed lawsuits or claims about to be filed showed that 37 percent covered non-recalled tires. In several of the foreign recalls, 16-inch tires were included (but are not recalled in the U.S.).

There are a number of documents and data that are still secret. This undermines public scrutiny of the scope of the August recall, and many of the documents are missing information or poorly formatted and so hard to read they look like first drafts. Secrecy is found in submissions by the companies to NHTSA, in documents not yet submitted, or gag orders in lawsuits that should be made public. The agency rarely uses its subpoena power authority but could do so to secure these protected documents. This may be painful for the companies, but it is essential given the broad public debate about this safety defect and the need for the companies to regain public trust. This information will probably leak out over time anyway, so it makes sense to release it now.

4. NHTSA failed to discover this defect because it lacks a proactive program to discover safety defects.

a. NHTSA was caught flatfooted in this case because it rarely pushes companies to obey the law. The Department allowed GM to resist recalling its five million defectively designed 1973–1987 pickup trucks with side-saddle gas tanks that explode in side-impact crashes (approximately 800 people have died because of fire in crashes with these vehicles, according to NHTSA's Fatal Accident Reporting System). It allowed Ford to resist recalling its vehicles equipped with ignition modules that frequently failed, causing vehicles to stall. It allowed Chrysler to label its correction of its minivans with defective rear-door latches that pop open in rear crashes, (throwing occupants outside), a "service campaign" and not a safety recall. I don't think its subpoena power has been exercised in 20 years, and it rarely imposes penalties when it learns companies have slithered around its request to produce documents, which unfortunately happens with some frequency.

Auto manufacturers roll the dice in attempts to avoid mandatory recalls and usually win. This time their coverup was revealed by an enterprising investigative reporter at KHOU in Houston on February 7 and 10. This time they are the losers as the media spotlight forces the story of the sorry state of safety defect enforcement and manufacturer compliance with the law into the public consciousness.

b. NHTSA also has no early warning system in place and has not been proactive in requiring manufacturer warnings or in using sources of information that are on the pulse-beat of current real world information about vehicle performance. They can and should routinely get information from: auto repair facilities; fleet owners, including national, state and local fleets; lawyers representing deceased and injured family members who find out about defects through discovery and cross examination of manufacturers; insurance company data; and also from the companies themselves, as they are the first to receive consumer complaints and dealer concerns. The auto companies also know, as in this case, the design decisions they have made that could compromise safety.

In this case, State Farm Insurance Co., the nation's largest insurer, sent an e-mail and called NHTSA in 1998 about 21 cases of Firestone tire tread separations, but the agency ignored it. The press reports that another 30 cases were discussed with the agency in 1999, and the agency ignored them as well. Finally, on April 25, 2000, in response to a NHTSA request, 70 reports covering 1996 through April 2000 were sent. How could this happen? How often does the agency check complaints dutifully filed by consumers through its hotline and in letters to spot trends? They are all on a computer list by make, model and alleged defect. Even if this happens routinely, it's not enough—because, as this case illustrates, most consumers don't bother contacting government agencies.

The agency should require, as does EPA, that a company notify the agency if it gets 25 complaints about the same alleged defect, and require, as does the Consumer Product Safety Commission, that the company notify the agency if three or more lawsuits alleging the same safety defect are filed.

The agency has also used a highly inappropriate system for evaluating whether a safety defect exists—looking at statistical data which are rarely adequate. If it cannot establish a statistical basis, the agency does not find a defect. Crash statistics are totally inadequate to justify such an approach. Yet, the Administrator admitted in testimony last week that NHTSA did something similar in this case—comparing 46 complaint problems to 40 million tires manufactured and didn't act. But with a catastrophic, deadly failure, this is completely inappropriate. And the agency never did the simple analysis published on Friday, September 8, in *The New York Times* showing that fatal crashes in 1995–1998 Ford Explorers are "nearly three times as likely to be tire related as fatalities involving other sport utilities or cars." The courts have held in a number of cases that if a safety element of the vehicle fails and can result in death or injury, there is a failure of safety performance sufficient to find a defect, and there is no need to look for dead bodies on the highway first.

The 1994 Michelin tire case reported in the *Akron Beacon Journal* is a different example. It was opened by NHTSA on the basis of five complaints with no injuries. The agency said it launched the investigation as a courtesy to the Kentucky Attorney General but says the complaints alone did not warrant it. But in testimony last week, NHTSA Administrator Sue Bailey said one seat belt complaint would be enough to open an investigation. Clearly the various elements of a case, not just the numbers, must be evaluated.

In short, NHTSA has not been the tough cop on the regulatory beat. When it is, the companies are more safety-conscious, the public is protected, and in the end it is less work for all parties. The Firestone/Ford case shows what happens when safety is not Job 1 in the companies or in the government.

5. Essential safety standards are severely out of date, were scrapped or delayed in the Reagan years, or are prohibited by law because of industry lobbying.

a. The tire safety standard is 32 years old and is not fully effective for testing radial tires. Both Ford and GM have recently stated that they favor an improved standard. The current standard tests for strength, endurance and how well the tire remains on the rim. Radial tires last much longer than bias ply tires and should be subjected to a tougher standard.

b. The Uniform Tire Quality Grading standard applies only to car tires, not truck/SUV tires. It is a consumer information requirement rating tread wear, traction and heat resistance with the rating molded into the tire. It should be expanded to cover truck/SUV tires. As it happens, the Explorer/Firestone tire is rated because it is used on a large Buick station wagon. For heat resistance, it gets the lowest grade. But Ford official Jon Harmon dismissed the poor rating, indicating that if the tire meets Ford's performance standards the C rating is of no concern. But Ford's tests have not been produced to date.

c. The roof crush standard is 30 years old. It is a static standard requiring weight to be placed on the roof of the vehicle (applied to SUVs beginning in model year 1994) equal to 1.5 times the maximum unloaded weight of the vehicle. In many of the Ford Explorer/Firestone rollover cases, the roof crushes into the vehicle, severely enhancing the likelihood of injury and death. A dynamic rollover crash worthiness standard should be issued addressing roof crush, door lock and hinges, side glazing materials, side air bags, and head protection. Crash protection in rollovers must include effective safety belts with pretensioners.

d. The first petition to NHTSA for a rollover prevention standard was filed by Representative Timothy Wirth 15 years ago. Others followed. In 1991 the Congress required NHTSA to conduct a rollover prevention rulemaking. The agency made an initial effort at developing a safety standard but then dropped it and instead proposed a consumer information requirement. The auto industry then got the Appropriations Committee to prohibit issuance of a consumer information rule until after a study by the National Academy of Sciences about the usefulness and presentation of consumer information. Finally in May 2000 the agency proposed to conduct New Car Assessment tests for rollover based on a static measurement of track width and center of gravity height, but once again the manufacturers objected and the Appropriations Committee bill requires yet another study by the NAS before it could be issued. This bill is now in conference.

Our coalition of consumer and health groups and insurers favors dropping the study and letting NHTSA proceed with its rulemaking on the consumer information test, even though we prefer a more comprehensive test. A 1998 Harris poll conducted for Advocates For Highway and Auto Safety shows 62 percent of the public wants such information. But we also want a rollover prevention standard. It is long overdue. About 9,500 highway deaths annually occur in rollover crashes—almost 25 percent of all highway deaths. This problem must be addressed, particularly with the large numbers of SUVs being used as family vehicles that are susceptible to rollover.

e. The agency should issue a rule for a tire inflation indicator on the dashboard, as I proposed 22 years ago. It was eliminated by the Reagan administration. The companies complain that tires are not properly inflated but then lobby to undercut consumers' ability to properly maintain their tires with accurate information.

f. The tire manufacturing information now molded into the black wall of the tire should be placed on the whitewall or outside of the tire so a consumer doesn't have to crawl under the car to find it to determine if their tire is subject to a recall. This was part of my rulemaking plan more than 20 years ago, but it was never issued after I left.

g. The tire reserve load consumer information requirement eliminated in the Reagan years should be reestablished to inform consumers of the maximum rated load capacity of the vehicle, so they know when they should inflate their tires for maximum load carrying.

h. The agency should be alert in this case to whether its requirement for record retention of only five years should be extended, since the critical evidence in this case extends over a decade.

i. Three elements of legislation are needed that are relevant to this case:

First, the 1982 legislation eliminating the responsibility of independent tire dealers to report the names and addresses of tire purchasers to the manufacturer for notification in the event of a recall should be changed back to requiring such record keeping as during the period from 1970 until 1982. Independent dealers with computers today can readily supply such names to the manufacturer. The current law only requires the independent dealer to give the consumer a card to mail themselves. A 1986 NHTSA report showed only 11 percent responded. Thus, in this case, most buyers from independent dealers will not be notified by mail.

Second, the current law requires tire owners to return the tire within 60 days of a recall notification (which, I presume, means if a manufacturer has no contact information, a consumer would have to rely on news reports) or 60 days after tire replacement. Car owners in recalls don't have this limitation. It is confusing enough to get tires replaced without this added complexity. It should be eliminated.

Third, the current prohibition in the law on a NHTSA rule requiring a continuous buzzer to alert occupants to buckle up should be eliminated. Among car companies, only Ford, I believe, now has a continuous buzzer. The current law only permits NHTSA to require a 4–8 second buzzer. Belt use is essential in rollovers. It should be encouraged in every way, including when the vehicle is in use.

Mr. Chairman, we urge the Committee to immediately mark-up and pass new legislative authority for NHTSA so it can do its job. It must be a priority for this Congress. And such legislation should instruct the agency to upgrade and issue the safety standards referenced above that are long overdue.

Thank you Mr. Chairman for the opportunity to testify on this important subject today.

Chronology of Firestone/Ford Knowledge of Tire Safety Defect

	1987
May 1, 1987	A Ford internal memo states that the stability of the Explorer [UN46] is worse than Bronco II and that it can be improved by widening, lowering and using a smaller P215 tire.
June 11, 1987	Ford internal memo on a meeting with Firestone reports that the ATX design is approved by Ford.
	1988
Fall 1988	Ford ADAMS reports states that the Explorer demonstrated "performance issues" at 35 psi but that they expected more favorable results at 26 psi.
November 25, 1988	An internal Ford Test Report shows Explorer lifts two wheels at 55 mph due to high center of gravity, tires and front suspension system.
	1989

Chronology of Firestone/Ford Knowledge of Tire Safety Defect—Continued

1989	Internal Ford document states that the cornering capacity of the Explorer is "[n]ot to exceed current [Bronco II] levels. Limit cornering capacity with larger tires through suspension revisions and tire pressure reduction." The document further discusses Tire Pressure Reduction: "Engineering has recommended use of tire pressures below maximum allowable inflation levels for all UN46 tires. As described previously, the reduced tire pressures increase understeer and reduce maximum cornering capacity (both "stabilizing" influences). This practice has been used routinely in heavy duty pickup truck and car station wagon applications to assure adequate understeer under all loading conditions. Nissan (Pathfinder), Toyota, Chevrolet, and Dodge also reduce tire pressures for selected applications. While we cannot be sure of their reasons, similarities in vehicle loading suggest that maintaining a minimal level of understeer under rear-loaded conditions may be the compelling factor."
January 11, 1989	An internal Ford memo reports a meeting with Firestone to discuss front suspension "jacking" on the Explorer and Bronco II, a phenomena that is "undesirable from a vehicle stability standpoint."
January 26, 1989	In an internal Ford memo, Ford engineers state the design goal [no two wheel lift] has not been met with the P235 ATX tire.
February 9, 1989	Ford hires Arvin Calspan to test the P245 tires. In a letter to James Avouris from George A. Tapia of the Arvin Calspan Tire Research Facility, Tapia reports that "[t]he P245 test tires at the 29 psi pressure condition showed a severe 'tread package' separation from the tire carcass."
February 20, 1989	In an internal Ford memo, Ford engineers recommend use of 26/26 psi along with various other spring changes due to stability testing showing two wheel lift with 35 psi.
March 2, 1989	Internal Firestone memo to Ford states that "in light of Ford's decision to specify 26 psi in the P245 tire for the Explorer, Firestone has tested the vehicle at 26 psi front and 35 psi rear" . . . "Calspan testing showed severe tread separation, but our testing used a more realistic procedure and we don't think it will be a problem."
April 5, 1989	An internal Ford memo reports that Consumer's Union told Mr. Sloan, Ford Vice President of Public Relations: "You have a real problem" with your Bronco II.
April 11, 1989	Failure Analysis memo [Roger McCarthy] makes a proposal to Ford's lawyers to conduct Consumer's Union testing.
April 21, 1989	An internal Ford memo from Sloan to upper management (including Red Poling) following meeting with Consumer's Union reports that Ford staff has "clouded their minds."
May 10, 1989	Ford Test Report reveals that J-turn results still show that the Explorer "rolls over" in 5 of 12 tests. Blazer and Bronco II do not roll over!
May 16, 1989	Internal Ford memo emphasizes the importance of how the Explorer performs in the Consumer's Union (avoidance maneuver) test and the need to return to Arizona for more testing.
May 17, 1989	Memo from Ford Truck Operations Management authorizes Consumer's Union testing in Arizona.
May 29, 1989	Internal Ford memo tells management that there is a "risk" that the Explorer "won't pass" the Consumer's Union test.
June 1989	*Consumer Reports* article tells consumers they should "avoid" the Bronco II.

Chronology of Firestone/Ford Knowledge of Tire Safety Defect—Continued

June 15, 1989	In an internal Ford memo to Truck Operations Management, Ford engineer Jim Mason recommends design changes to the Explorer: *Lists eight possible changes *Analyzes them to show effect on stability index *Analyzes them with regard to "timing" of Job 1 [they will delay Job 1]. *Indicates Consumers' Union results show Explorer is same as Bronco II *Says these design changes can make the Explorer as good as Blazer *Management recommends adopting as many as possible **without delaying Job 1.**
July 1989	Ford memo indicating that Ford lowered the front of the Explorer half an inch and stiffened the front springs to increase stability.
September 11, 1989	In an internal Ford email to Charles White, Roger Stornant states, "I believe that new info is that our competitors are recognizing CU Test as a requirement and have designed their new utility vehicles to meet. OGC is concerned we will be the only OEM with a vehicle that has a significant chance of failing the CU test. I believe that management is aware of the potential risk w/P235 tires and has accepted risk. CU test is generally unrepresentative of real world and I see no 'real' risk in failing except what may result in wave of spurious litigation."
September 12, 1989	In an internal Ford email to Charles White, Roger F. Stornant expresses that OGC is concerned that the UN46 [Explorer] would fail Consumers Union tests with the P235 tires. "Based on the variability of the test, as demonstrated by our own drivers, it is possible to pass the CU test with the P235 tires; however, if we were using the CU test as sign-off requirement, we would not accept this combination (P235 ATX & 2dr)."
December 1989	Internal memo states that Explorer with 235 tires set at 26 psi passed the rollover test.
	1990
February 1990	In order to meet the production deadline, Ford officials rejected some proposals to improve the stability of the Explorer (i.e. widening the track width).
March 1990	JOB 1: '91–'94 Explorer
May 1, 1990	Ford asks Firestone in a letter from Jim Avouris to issue a dealer bulletin regarding tire replacement, emphasizing the importance of using the correct size tire and the correct air pressures on the Explorer [due to rollover sensitivity].
September 12, 1990	In an email from Mazzola (Firestone) to Staples (Ford), Ford requests that Firestone (a) change the tire design to a low rolling resistance polymer and (b) change the tire pressure to 30/35 psi for a 1.6 mpg improvement on CAFE. The question is raised whether air pressure change will affect "vehicle dynamics," [i.e., rollover].
	1991
February 12, 1991	FILED: Woodburn v. Firestone Tire and Rubber Co.; et al. [injuries unknown]
February 14, 1991	In a memo from Dave Wotton at Ford to Reichenbach at Firestone with tire objectives for the 1995 model Explorer [UN105] shows that the goal is same traction, better rolling resistance and better wear properties. Timing is November 94.

Chronology of Firestone/Ford Knowledge of Tire Safety Defect—Continued

December 19, 1991	Firestone memo from Reichenbach to Gibas at Ford saying it is "increasingly important" that we know whether you will adopt the tire for the Explorer.
	1992
March 24, 1992	FILED: Johnson v. Nissan, et al. [injuries unknown]
April 23, 1992	FILED: Cherinka v. Ford; et al [Explorer/ATX tread separation; injuries unknown]
April 29, 1992	FILED: Roberston v. Firestone/Bridgestone, Inc.; et al. [injuries unknown]
May 10, 1992	Letter from T.A. Mast & R.M. Campbell of Ford to Bridgestone/Firestone, Michelin, Goodyear, and General Tire to revise UPN105 Tire Targets. The primary objectives were to maintain tire wear, traction, and maximize rolling resistance.
June 16, 1992	Internal Ford memo entitled "Targets—UN105" contains: *"*CANDIDATE TIRE*—P235/75R15 SL ALL TERRAIN OWL" *"*NOTE: Primary importance should be placed on the 67″ drum rolling resistance.*" *"Tire pressure—30 PSI for Ranger 4X4" *"Tire pressure—26 PSI for Explorer"
August 27, 1992	Memo from J.E. Behr of Firestone to R.D. Bacigalupi, Ford Light Truck Engineering, answering questions from Ford about changing the design of the ATX to use a different tread compound for rolling resistance improvement.
	1993
September 28, 1993	A memo from Reichenbach at Firestone to Skyner at Ford asks to evaluate a tire wear concern on the 10K testing as the '95 Explorer is exhibiting right front inside shoulder wear.
December 22, 1993	FILED: Blackaller v. Ford; Firestone; et al. [2 injuries, 2 deaths]
	1994
April 12, 1994	Ford Light Truck Operations Tire Construction Detail Sheet specifies the P235/75R15 tire at a maximum psi of 35.
September 9, 1994	FILED: Dreher v. Ford, et al. [injuries unknown]
1995	Ford/Firestone begins shipping 16″ Wilderness tire to Saudi Arabia.
	1995
February 23, 1995	FILED: Greenwald v. Bridgestone/Firestone, Inc.; Ford; et al. [Explorer/ATX separation; injuries unknown]
August 7, 1995	FILED: Ellis v. Bridgestone/Firestone, Inc.; Ford; et al. [Explorer/ATX; injuries unknown]
August 7, 1995	FILED: Dickson v. Bridgestone/Firestone, Inc.; et al. [Explorer/ATX separation from Wilson, NC plant; injuries unknown]
	1996
January 4, 1996	FILED: Combs v. Ford [Bronco II/ATX separation; 1 fatality]
March 13, 1996	Welch v. Ford; et al. [Explorer/ATX separation; 3 injuries] (incident date)

Chronology of Firestone/Ford Knowledge of Tire Safety Defect—Continued

June 20, 1996	A memo from Arizona Game and Fish Department wildlife manager Lowell Whitaker to his regional supervisor describes two blow outs of Firestone tires. "During the past few months I have been cautioned as a user of Firestone tires by DPS (Department of Public Safety) that there have been a series of accidents caused by the separation of the tread from the tire on Firestone tires."
July 1996	FILED: Rogers v. Ford; et al. [Explorer/ATX separation; 1 injury, 1 fatality]
July 12, 1996	A memo from Deputy Yuma County (Arizona) Attorney John K. White regarding Firestone Firehawk ATX tires reported: "Some tires of this model have had their tread separate from the body of the tire." "Firestone is aware of the problem and will be replacing tires where needed. (A shipment of tires is currently on its way for various Sheriff's vehicles.)" "It is strongly recommended that you do not drive vehicles equipped with these tires at 'freeway speeds' (or at all, if possible) until you have them . . . evaluated."
July 22, 1996	Letter from Robert J. Descheemaker at the Arizona State Procurement Office to Roger Abrams of Bridgestone/Firestone requesting replacement of all Firehawk ATX tires bought under state contracts.
August 19, 1996	Ford CQIS computer report on Explorer with 20k miles—Colonial Ford dealer in Danbury, Connecticut has 16 Explorers with distorted tires like this—belt is obviously distorted and about to separate
August 26, 1996	FILED: Gauvain v. Bridgestone Corporation; et al. [Explorer/ATX separation; 1 fatality]
September 23, 1996	FILED: Brizendine v. So. New. T.B.A. Supply Co., et al. [injuries unknown]
December 27, 1996	FILED: Guara v. Ford, et al [Bronco II/ATX separation; injuries unknown]
	1997
January 17, 1997	FILED: Kehm v. Bridgestone/Firestone, Inc.; et al. [Bronco/ATX separation; 3 injuries]
February 21, 1997	FILED: Spivak v. Bridgestone/Firestone, Inc.; et al. [Explorer/ATX separation; injuries unknown]
June 1997	Speed rating on tires in Venezuela changed from R [106 mph] to S [112 mph], with tires to be made in Venezuela.
June 1997	FILED: State Farm Mutual Automobile Insurance Company v. Bridgestone/Firestone, Inc. [injuries unknown]
June 2, 1997	FILED: Stephens v. Catherine A. Broome and Christopher D. Kehm; Bridgestone/Firestone; et al. [Bronco/ATX separation; 3 injuries]
June 11, 1997	Fax from Daryl G. Parma of Firestone to Luis Abreau states that tests show "how much better" the Wilderness AT (ST381J) is than the ATX II (SR897J) which would replace the ATX II.
July 28, 1997	FILED: Jackson v. Bridgestone/Firestone, Inc.; Ford; et al. [Explorer/ATX separation; 3 injuries, 1 fatality]
August 1997	An undated memo states Ford and Firestone are notified of tire problems in Saudi Arabia [from the Congressional notebooks]

Chronology of Firestone/Ford Knowledge of Tire Safety Defect—Continued

August 7, 1997	FILED: Lazarus v. Bridgestone/Firestone, Inc.; et al. [Explorer/ATX separation; injuries unknown]
September 16, 1997	FILED: Silva v. Ford; et al. [Explorer/ATX separation; injuries unknown]
September 22, 1997	FILED: Carrillo v. Bridgestone/Firestone, Inc.; et al. [Blazer/ATX separation; 2 fatalities]
October 7, 1997	FILED: Flores v. Ford; Bridgestone/Firestone, et al. [Explorer/ATX separation; injuries unknown]
October 21, 1997	FILED: Chinichian v. Bridgestone/Firestone, Inc.; et al. [Explorer/ATX separation; injuries unknown]
December 1, 1997	FILED: Ortiz v. Bridgestone/Firestone, Inc.; Ford; et al. [Explorer/ATX separation; 1 fatality]
	1998
January 1998	Glenn R. Drake, regional marketing manager in the United Arab Emirates for Ford expresses concern about Firestone's response to the tire problems in an email to other Ford executives: "If this was a single case, I would accept Firestone's response as they are the experts in the tire business, case closed. However, we now have three cases and it is possible that Firestone is not telling us the whole story to protect them from a recall or a lawsuit."
January 9, 1998	FILED: Haffey v. Ford; et al. [Explorer/ATX separation; 2 injuries, 1 fatality]
January 22, 1998	FILED: Huffman v. Ford; et al [Explorer/ATX separation; 2 injuries, 1 fatality]
January 28, 1998	FILED: Bragg v. Bridgestone/Firestone, Inc.; et al. [1 injury]
April 23, 1998	FILED: Van Etten v. Bridgestone/Firestone, Inc.; Ford [Explorer/ATX separation; 3 injuries, 1 fatality]
April 24, 1998	FILED: Parra v. Ford; et al. [Explorer/Wilderness HT; 2 injuries]
May 15, 1998	FILED: Kim v. Ford; et al. [Explorer/ATX separation; 2 injuries, 2 fatalities]
June 24, 1998	In an internal Bridgestone/Firestone interoffice memo to M. Hamaya Firestone, K. Ball acknowledges that P235/75R15 ATX II separation is 92.8% of all ATX II claims and 53.6% of all Firestone light truck claims for the year of 1997. Additionally, warranty claims on ATX II tires jumped from 42 in 1995 to 279 in 1997, a sixfold increase. 1998 light truck claims are 469 for separations and 8 for road hazards. 1997 light truck claims by plant for the ATX II show 117 for Decatur, 101 for Wilson, and 51 for Joliette.
July 13, 1998	FILED: Simmons v. Ford; et al [Explorer/ATX separation; 2 injuries]
July 22, 1998	In an email to William Duckwitz at NHTSA from State Farm Associate Research Administrator Samuel Boyden, Boyden advises NHTSA of 21 Firestone ATX P235/75R15 tire failures causing injuries. Fourteen cases were in 1991–1995 Ford Explorers. The problem was dismissed as "unremarkable" by NHTSA.
July 31, 1998	FILED: Gutierrez v. Bridgestone/Firestone [Explorer/ATX separation; injuries unknown]
August 27, 1998	FILED: Lockwood v. Bridgestone/Firestone, Inc.; Ford; et al. [Explorer/ATX separation; 1 fatality]

Chronology of Firestone/Ford Knowledge of Tire Safety Defect—Continued

September 17, 1998	FILED: Alvarez v. Bridgestone/Firestone, Inc.; et al. [Explorer/ATX separation; injuries unknown]
October 24, 1998	Ford Dealer Paul Wright, Technical Branch Manager, Al Jazirah Vehicles, expresses concern and frustrations in a letter to John W. Thompson, Tamimi Company Commercial Division that despite his warning about the safety of the tires, he did not receive a response and was being "kept in the dark to what is happening." "As you know, this concern goes back to mid-1997 when we first notified you of this concern. I have to state that I believe this situation to be of a safety concern, which could endanger both the vehicle and more importantly the user of the vehicle. So I am asking what is going on? Do we have to have a fatality before any action is taken of this subject?" "I would recommend to ensure that we do not have any further incidents regarding tyres that Firestone RECALL all 1995/1996/1997 explorers fitted with this type of tyre, as this is a safety related concern."
1999	Federal data from the Fatal Accident Reporting System for 1995–98 was available to Ford, Firestone, and NHTSA showing that Explorer fatalities were almost three times as likely to be tire related as those with other SUVs or cars and that Explorer crashes increased significantly in the late 1990s compared with other SUVs.
	1999
January 1999 or after	Explorer Tire DNP—Exposed Findings of Tire Explosion and Car Rolling Due to Tire Inflation. Notes report of 22 Firestone and 10 Goodyear tread separations and rollover crashes.
January 12, 1999	FILED: Hill v. Bridgestone/Firestone, Inc. [5 injuries]
January 19, 1999	FILED: Wieters v. Bridgestone/Firestone, Inc.; et al. [injuries unknown]
January 22, 1999	An email from D.J. Candido, to Firestone colleagues concluded that for countries prone to heat induced separation, the Wilderness HT, with European specs, was the best application choice. However, they also acknowledged that this model is more prone to chip and tear. The best choice is to develop a new tire with similar heat specs to the European model and similar chip/tear specs to the Australian model.
January 27, 1999	In an interoffice Bridgestone/Firestone memo entitled P255/79R16 Wilderness AT Adjustment Data to Bruce Halverson, Market Quality Engineer, Nashville, Luis E. Abreu, Technical Service Manager, Firestone Venezuela, indicates that 47 tires in Venezuela had tread or belt separation. Of these 47, 34 had international serial codes and 13 had DOT (USA) code. In an attachment, Abreu further notes the most critical defects from January 1995 to December 1998 are Tread leaving casing (135), Belt leaving belt (136), Breaker leaving casing (137), shoulder separation between rubber and casing (230), belt edge separation (235).
January 28, 1999	In an email to Melanie Gumz, Glenn Drake of Ford reports that he is suspicious of Firestone's response to the problem and suggests that Firestone is not telling the entire story in order to protect themselves from lawsuits and a recall. Drake also questions the durability of the product and the fact that Ford is about to change the tire on all Explorers and Mountaineers to a tire that has better high speed durability. Drake recommends that Ford conduct its own analysis in order to protect Ford and give the dealers and customers an independent opinion. "[W]e owe it to our customers and our shareholders to investigate this for our own peace of mind."

Chronology of Firestone/Ford Knowledge of Tire Safety Defect—Continued

January 1999	In a memo to Firestone Distribution entitled Ford Explorer—Concerns in the Middle East (P255/70R16), John E. Behr, Account Executive for Original Equipment Tire Sales, reported, "I attempted to assure the Ford people that we are not aware of any defect with these tires, and that we've supplied over 1.1 million of the same tires to Ford over the past three years (1996 thru 1998) for usage in North America, with excellent field performances."
January 29, 1999	In a memo to Bridgestone/Firestone Distribution, John E. Behr, OE Sales, expresses that Ford is concerned that the tires in the Middle East are defective. Raises the issue of using the P255/70R16 Wilderness HT BSW H instead of the P255/70R16 was requested by Ford. He advised that the H tire would be better suited for high speed driving and more resistant to heat buildup but would not be more puncture resistant.
February 8, 1999	FILED: Menendez v. Ford, Bridgestone/Firestone, Inc.; et al. [Explorer/ATX separation; injuries unknown]
February 14, 1999	In a letter to Keshav Das, Technical Service Department of Firestone at Dubai, John Garthwaite, Ford National Service Director, Al Jazirah Vehicles (Ford Dealer in the Middle East), warns Bridgestone/Firestone of the serious nature of the problem with P255/70/R16 AT tires. Garthwaite indicates that an accident occurred with a tire at 30 psi. The tread separated completely and the tire remained inflated. Garthwiate expressed his strong conviction that there is a "distinct problem with all or at least a certain production run of this particular tyre."
February 25, 1999	Garthwaite continues to question the safety of the P255/70/R16 tire in a subsequent letter to Keshav Das. "These incidents involving Firestone P255/70/R16 tyres is beginning to become an epidemic." He further states that "Nothing in your reply has done anything to re-assure me that there may not exist a defect in a particular batch of your product . . ."
March 11, 1999	An internal Bridgestone/Firestone Letter to S. Katsura, et. al. from Firestone Account Executive, John E. Behr expresses concern over the result of Ford's proposed consumer notification program and its potential effects and "perception" it would convey in Saudi Arabia as well as "complications it could create in North America." The letter also indicates that other Ford people also disfavored the notification program. Ford planned to change the tire in the Middle East to the H-rated European tire that is more heat resistant.
March 12, 1999	An internal Ford memo to Dave MacKinnon from Church Seilnacht states the following: "John [Behr] also reaffirmed that the "H" rated tire is the most resistant to damage from underinflated operation." "Firestone legal has some major reservations about the plan to notify customers and offer them an option. First, they feel that the U.S. D.O.T. will have to be notified of the program, since the same product is sold in the U.S. Second, they are afraid that the Saudi government will see this as a recall and react dramatically, including prohibiting the import of the current OEM tire. They believe the best course of action for the vehicles already in the market is to handle the tire issues on a case-by-case basis." "Related to the Firestone legal concerns is the possibility that we will be expanding the owner relations issue. The owners who receive the notification letter may see the program as a recall and not be willing to pay anything to upgrade the tires. So, instead of 8 owner relations issues, we now have X times as many." "I [talked to] Corey MacGillivray in the OGC last Monday about the proposal. He didn't think that working on a case-by-case basis with the owners of the damaged vehicles presented a problem, but he was concerned about the implications of the owner letter (similar to the Firestone concerns)."

Chronology of Firestone/Ford Knowledge of Tire Safety Defect—Continued

April 27, 1999	FILED: Glick v. Firestone Tire and Service Center, et al. [Explorer/ATX separation; injuries unknown]
April 28, 1999	Ford memo on Firestone Tire Tread Separations states that Ford will "address the issues related to the rollovers on a case-by-case basis."
May 4, 1999	FILED: Healy v. Bridgestone/Firestone, Inc. [Explorer/ATX separation; 1 injury]
May 4, 1999	FILED: Patterson (Elroy) v. Bridgestone/Firestone [injuries unknown]
May 4, 1999	In a fax from Arabian Car Marketing to Ford Middle East and North Africa Company, Oman Ford advises Ford Middle East that it is replacing Firestone tires with Michelin tires prior to delivery because Explorer users are becoming aware of (through the internet) the off-road limitations of the Explorer.
June 24, 1999	FILED: Jenkins v. Bridgestone/Firestone, Inc. [injuries unknown]
June 30, 1999	Fax labeled "Top Urgent & Very Important" to Ford Middle East from Arabian Car Marketing Company warns Ford Middle East and North Africa that the tires are failing: "news of fatal accidents on Explorer is spreading rapidly." "The tire problem has already resulted in a severe decline in Explorer sales." "We are also worried about further fatalities and possible lawsuits."
July 2, 1999	FILED: Jenkins v. Bridgestone/Firestone, Inc. [injuries unknown]
July 7, 1999	FILED: Meza v. McCombs HFC Limited D/B/A Red, et al. [Explorer/ATX separation; injuries unknown]
July 16, 1999	FILED: Progressive County Mutual Insurance Company v. Bridgestone/Firestone, Inc. [Explorer/ATX separation; injuries unknown]
July 28, 1999	FILED: Jarvis v. Bridgestone/Firestone, Inc. [Explorer/ATX separation; injuries unknown]
July 30, 1999	FILED: Taylor v. Bridgestone/Firestone, Inc. [Explorer/ATX separation; injuries unknown]
August 2–5, 1999	Teams from Ford and Bridgestone/Firestone recognize Ford Explorer rollover due to tread leaving casing in the *Venezuelan Tire Survey* of problem tires. Suggested possible causes are excessive speed (173 Km/hr (26 Km in 9 minutes)), heavy load (8 passengers plus luggage), and high pavement temperature (55 degrees Celsius at 1:20 pm). Suggested possible results were tire fatigue and separations. 132 tires inspected at dealers in 4 locations revealed 8 underinflated tires (Wilderness P255/70R/16AT and P235/75R/15ATX) The teams suggested as one of the possible actions to improve the circumstances in Venezuela, increasing the recommended inflation pressure on the vehicle from 28 to 30 in the front and from 26 to 30 in the back. The 30 psi standard was considered to be the USA standard of inflation.
August 6, 1999	FILED: Aoyagi v. Bridgestone/Firestone, Inc.; et al. [injuries unknown]
August 9, 1999	Letter from B.V. Halverson to Mr. J. Gonzalez of Bridgestone Firestone acknowledges that "sustained high speed driving must be considered as a normal input in the performance of vehicles and tires in Venezuela." Mr. Carlos Maren "really wanted a BFS recommendation that would guarantee that a tire would never have a separation."
August 12, 1999	FILED: Romero v. Bridgestone/Firestone, Inc.; et al. [Explorer/ATX separation; injuries unknown]

Chronology of Firestone/Ford Knowledge of Tire Safety Defect—Continued

August 13, 1999	FILED: Jimenez v. Bridgestone/Firestone, Inc. [Explorer/ATX separation; injuries unknown]
August 17, 1999	Ford begins replacing tires on Saudi Explorers through a "customer notification enhancement action" and not a "recall." Excerpts from correspondences regarding the "Owner Notification Program" "Unique GCC usage patterns, environmental conditions and maintenance practices may result in tire degradation and potentially, tread separation. Nineteen rollovers, fourteen fatalities and ten injuries are alleged to have been attributed to this condition." "Approximately 6,800 1995–99 MY Explorer and Mountaineer vehicles produced at the Louisville Assembly Plant from Job 1, 1995, through July 30, 1999, are potentially affected." "Based on the Field Review Committee recommendation, a field action has been approved to request owners to return potentially affected vehicles to dealers for replacement of the Firestone Wilderness brand tires with Goodyear Wrangler brand tires."
August 19, 1999	FILED: De Leon v. Bridgestone/Firestone, Inc.; et al. [injuries unknown]
August 23, 1999	In a letter to owners of light truck vehicles, Bridgestone/Firestone offers free tire inspection and free rotation service as a special offer to Venezuelan owners of light truck vehicles.
August 27, 1999	In a letter to C.E. Mazzorin, Ford's L.A. Klein indicates that the tire problems in the Middle East are largely due to the fact that the tire was not designed for the Middle Eastern market. The tire's speed rating is "S" which allows for speeds up to 112 mph. The Middle East requires higher speed ratings.
September 1999	In a letter to it's GCC dealers, Ford stated: "Ford and Firestone have been working to identify a Firestone tire that we can recommend that may offer a greater margin of resistance to puncture and or tread separation for the conditions unique to the GCC region than the current tire. That tire has been identified as the 'special service' tire currently available only in the Saudi Arabian market. This tire is more puncture resistant than the current production tire."
Fall 1999	Ford began replacing Firestone tires on Explorers in ten Middle East countries.
September 1, 1999	FILED: Hendricks v. Bridgestone/Firestone, Inc. [Explorer/ATX separation; injuries unknown]
September 3, 1999	FILED: Bean v. Bridgestone/Firestone, Inc.; et al. [Explorer/ATX separation; injuries unknown]
September 9, 1999	FILED: Porsche v. Ford, Bridgestone/Firestone, Inc. [3 injuries]
September 12, 1999	In a letter from John Garthwaite, National Service Director, Al Jazirah Vehicles, Saudi Arabia, to David MacKinnon, Director of Ford Customer Service, Dubai, Garthwaite once again advises of tread separation problems in Saudi Arabia. He suggests an in-depth Firestone tire investigation. "I am afraid that I can see a pattern emerging here. The tyre in this second case is totally destroyed but it is clear to me that the body damage is indicative of tread separation in the first instance."
September 13, 1999	FILED: Smith v. Bridgestone/Firestone, Inc.; et al. [injuries unknown]

Chronology of Firestone/Ford Knowledge of Tire Safety Defect—Continued

September 14, 1999	Ford memo entitled "1995/99 Explorer/Mountaineer Firestone P255/70R16 Tire Separation in the United States" states: "While driving vehicle, the tire tread separated from the main carcass of the tire. The tire failure is discovered when the driver hears the tire tread hitting the wheel house or the tire goes flat." "MORS (Master Owners Relation System)—Reviewed all 95/99 MORS reports (4236) for tires and wheels. Found 32 'possible' tread separation claims on Firestone (22) and Goodyear (10). 3 of the 32 possible claims were for the P225/70R15 tire from Firestone. 10 of the 32 possible claims were for the P235/75R15 tire from Goodyear. 18 of the 32 possible claims were for the P235/75R15 tire from Firestone."
September 15, 1999	Internal Ford memo from Carlos Mazzorin to Jac Nasser and others: The attachment dated August 27, 1999 states: "Issue description: While driving the vehicle at high speeds, for prolonged periods of time, the tire tread separated (belt edge separation) from the main carcass of the tire. 19 rollovers attributed to this issue have occurred in Saudi Arabia, Oman and Qatar combined. Several fatalities have resulted. The issue has also occurred in Venezuela, and fatalities have also resulted in that market. No known instances have occurred in other markets." "Ford first became aware of the issue in GCC markets in December 1998." In Venezuela, Ford "discovered the issue in early Spring 1999."
September 17, 1999	FILED: Douglas v. Ford; Bridgestone/Firestone; et al. [Explorer/ATX separation; injuries unknown]
October 1, 1999	Interoffice memo from L.A. Klein to C.E. Mazzorin reveals Ford's admission that it was responsible for choosing to use the North American tire in the GCC (Gulf Countries) market and determines the tire was not suitable for this area. Firestone was not part of that decision. *GCC Market:* *"Negotiations with Firestone have stopped. Firestone's position that the tire meets all quoted functional specifications, and that it was not meant for the GCC market application is confirmed by our research. It appears that Ford chose to use the North American specified tire in the GCC market, and Firestone was not part of that decision." Ford also indicates that the tires failing in Venezuela were specifically designed for the Venezuelan market and therefore the responsibility lies with Firestone.
October 19, 1999	Report entitled 1999 Firestone Quarterly Meeting: Critical Performance Issues, Aiken, SC indicates that tire separations were up to 3365 from 2929. Belt edge separation up 18.3%, belt leaving belt was up 10.1%, and SW separation—rubber from casing was up 63.6% for 1999 third quarter compared to 1998. This report does not separate out the individual tires. Firestone Adjustment Performance—Service Group states that more improvement in separations are needed to reduce LT REC adjustments. Firestone Adjustment Performance of major lines indicated that Wilderness AT and Wilderness HT experienced increases in adjustments related to Ford F150 sizes. The adjustment analysis also indicates that Firestone Light Truck—recreational experienced an increase in belt edge separation (up 22.3%), belt leave belt (up 11.1%), and SW SEP—Rubber from casing (up 69.6%).
October 19, 1999	The Radial ATXII also experienced a 5.2% increase in belt edge separation. Firestone report indicates that Decatur plant experiences substantial number of problems compared to the other plants.

Chronology of Firestone/Ford Knowledge of Tire Safety Defect—Continued

November 10, 1999	FILED: Guillen v. Bridgestone/Firestone, Inc., et al. [injuries unknown]
December 21, 1999	FILED: Gilmore v. Bridgestone/Firestone; et al. [injuries unknown]
	2000
2000	1999 vs. 1998 Adjustments data, Firestone revealed that Wilderness tire separations increased 194% and Wilderness adjustments are "growing quickly."
2000 est.	In a Firestone document "Explorer Tire DNP" giving status report: "In July 1997 FoV representatives were called to a meeting in Caracas with a group of independent lawyers representing four (4) customers. The objective of this meeting as expressed by these lawyers, was to draw Ford attention to a situation related to their customers, but that they felt could be greater." "High incidence of vehicle rollover after a tire blowout or tread loss has not been detected for other vehicle brands: Toyota, GM, and Chrysler all have significant market presence in this market segment."
January 1, 2000	In a Bridgestone/Firestone 1999 Year End Minor Profit Loss Report from William Thomas to Dave Laubie, attached charts show 1998 and 1999 data on tire tread separations by tire type and plant indicating large numbers of tread separations in tires manufactured at Decatur plant and with 235/75R15 tire. Also shows increasing claims for SXR4S Tire in 1999. Overall separation are up 10 in 1999 over 1998. 25% of total separations in 1999 were ATX II.
February 2000	Ford offers free replacement tires for vehicles in Malaysia and Thailand.
February 2000	Officials from Bridgestone/Firestone were briefed as early as February about rising warranty costs for the now recalled tires according to internal Bridgestone/Firestone documents including a series of charts distributed at a sales meeting in February, 2000. One chart tracking "separations increasing" revealed that the number of warranty claims for tread separation had risen from 4,200 in 1998 to 4,694 in 1999 (an increase of 11.8 percent). Another chart stated that "Wilderness AT needs improvement." While still other charts analyzed patterns in tread separations emphasizing tires for light trucks. These charts revealed that the number of tread separations involving Wilderness tires had risen 144 percent from 1998 to 1999.
February 7, 2000 & Feb. 10, 2000	KHOU, CBS affiliate station in Houston, breaks story of significant numbers of deaths and lawsuits with Firestone tires on Ford Explorers. Firestone Statement on February 4 before the programs aired says: "The Radial ATX has proved to be a reliable workhorse for U.S. consumers. Our experience with the Radial ATX indicates high consumer satisfaction with the quality and reliability of these tires. No court or jury has ever found any deficiency in these tires."
February 10, 2000	In a letter from Christine Karbowiak, Vice President, Public Affairs, Firestone, to Robert Decherd, Chairman, President and CEO of A.H. Belo Corp., and Peter Diaz, President and General Manager of KHOU-TV, Firestone states that KHOU-TV's broadcast series regarding its tires, "contains falsehoods and misrepresentations that improperly disparage Firestone and its product, the Radial ATX tire." It further asserts, "This series has unmistakably delivered the false messages that Radial ATX tires are dangerous, that they threaten the safety of anyone using them, and that they should be removed from every vehicle on which they are installed. Each of these messages is simply untrue."
February 25, 2000	Bridgestone/Firestone report indicates that separations in Wilderness tires are on the rise, but ATX are decreasing.

Chronology of Firestone/Ford Knowledge of Tire Safety Defect—Continued

March 5, 2000	NHTSA ODI resume (IE00–016=different from current investigation file number) indicates 22 complaints, 8 crashes, and 4 fatalities due to tire tread separation. (All ODI complaints are sent to company when received.)
March 6, 2000	NHTSA opens preliminary inquiry after KHOU-TV programs prompted consumer complaints.
March 22, 2000	Firestone survey of 243 tires on 63 vehicles that were trade-ins or lease return vehicles shows that 31% of the 15″ tires were under-inflated and 51% of the 16″ tires were under-inflated and at total of 9 tires had less than 20 psi.
April 25, 2000	In response to a request from NHTSA, Samuel Boyden, State Farm Associate Research Administrator, emailed a breakdown by calendar year and tire type (Firestone ATX, ATX II, and Wilderness tires) for the period covering 1996 to April 2000. This contained information on 70 reports.
May 2000	Ford offers to replace tires for customers in Colombia, Ecuador and Venezuela.
May 2000	Ford shifts to Goodyear tires in Venezuela as it waits for a U.S. Firestone response. Ford's action covers about 39,800 vehicles.
May 2, 2000	NHTSA opens investigation of 47 million ATX, ATX II, and Wilderness Firestone tires (investigation number PE00–020) with 90 complaints reporting 33 crashes including 4 fatal crashes and 17 injury crashes resulting in 27 injuries and 4 fatalities. Unknown to NHTSA, lawsuits and notices of intent to file involved at least 35 fatalities and 130 injuries.
May 8, 2000	NHTSA sends a list of interrogatories to Bridgestone/Firestone as part of its investigation of the tire failures. NHTSA requests that Firestone respond by June 19th.
May 10, 2000	NHTSA sends a list of interrogatories to Ford as part of its investigation of the tire failures. NHTSA requests that Ford respond by June 23rd.
June 6, 2000	Internal Ford Memo lists 21 vehicles sold in Gulf Countries. Lists Explorer (in Venezuela) psi at 28/28 for the 15″ tire. The new 15″ tires are listed at 30/30.
June 16, 2000	Ford requests an extension of the deadline to respond to NHTSA's interrogatories with an anticipated completion date of October 13th.
June 19, 2000	Ford requests extension from NHTSA for full response.
June 20, 2000	In response to NHTSA's interrogatories, Bridgestone/Firestone submits a partial response.
June 22, 2000	NHTSA grants Bridgestone/Firestone an extension until August 14th to provide information in response to its interrogatories.
July 24, 2000	In response to NHTSA's interrogatories, Ford submits a partial response.
July 25, 2000	After a story aired on KCBS regarding Ford Explorers and ATX tires, Firestone instructed dealers to replace tires with Bridgestone or Firestone tires of the customer's choice. However, "[t]his sale should be a regular sales ticket. Do not use an adjustment ticket." [Adjustments (warranties) are used by NHTSA and industry to track defects.]
July 31, 2000	Public learns of Ford's replacement of Firestone tires on Explorers in Venezuela.
July 31, 2000	Public learns of Ford's replacement of Firestone tires on Explorers overseas.

Chronology of Firestone/Ford Knowledge of Tire Safety Defect—Continued

July 31, 2000	Ford submits another partial response to NHTSA's original interrogatories.
August 2, 2000	NHTSA reports it is probing 21 deaths in crashes of pickup trucks and SUVs where tire failure may have played a role.
August 4, 2000	Sears, Roebuck & Co., the No. 1 tire retailer, stops selling certain Firestone tires.
August 4, 2000	Ford submits another partial response to NHTSA's original interrogatories.
August 6, 2000	Firestone announces a "customer information notice" in Venezuela in which certain models of tires would be replaced.
August 7, 2000	NHTSA announces investigation of 46 deaths related to the Firestone tires. Discount tire and Montgomery Ward suspend sales of Firestone tires until more information is made available.
August 9, 2000	Firestone/Bridgestone voluntarily recalls 6.5 million 15″ ATX, ATX II, and Wilderness AT from the Decatur plant. (14.4 manufactured)
August 14, 2000	Bridgestone/Firestone asks NHTSA to again extend its deadline to respond to NHTSA's initial interrogatories until September 5th.
August 15, 2000	NHTSA raises the number of traffic deaths linked to Firestone tires from 46 to 62. It is also looking into reports of 100 injuries.
August 18, 2000	Ford's partial response to NHTSA's inquiries.
August 28, 2000	Bridgestone announces a boost in replacement production to 650,000.
August 29, 2000	NHTSA requests supplemental information from Ford as part of its ongoing investigation of the Firestone tire failures. NHTSA requests that Ford respond by September 31st.
August 31, 2000	Venezuela's consumer protection agency asked prosecutors to bring criminal charges against both Bridgestone/Firestone and Ford. Ford's Jac Nasser responded by stating, "The accusation from the Venezuelan government that Ford Venezuela lied is absolutely unfounded." Venezuelan authorities contend that Ford and Firestone held secret meetings to determine what was wrong following the first reports of incidents in 1998. Instead of instituting a recall, officials allege that Ford asked Firestone to redesign the Wilderness tire.
August 31, 2000	NHTSA raises to 88 from 62 the number of deaths associated with the Firestone tires. Venezuelan consumer agency, Indecu, recommends that Ford and Firestone be prosecuted for 46 deaths related to the tires in Venezuela.
September 1, 2000	Firestone declines NHTSA's request to voluntarily expand recall to 1.4 million tires not included in the original recall. NHTSA issues consumer advisory on additional 1.4 million Firestone tires. NHTSA states that some of the tires have "high tread separation rates."
September 4, 2000	Bridgestone/Firestone issues a recall in Venezuela of 62,000 Venezuelan-made 15-inch and 16-inch Wilderness tires. Previously, only US-manufactured tires were being replaced.
September 4, 2000	Bridgestone/Firestone reaches agreement with union to settle labor disputes and avert a strike at nine U.S. plants.
September 6, 2000	Mr. Wyant, Firestone Vice President of Quality Assurance, testified that, "They [Ford] see every bit of the field performance data that is devoted to approving a tire."

Chronology of Firestone/Ford Knowledge of Tire Safety Defect—Continued

September 6, 2000	The Senate Appropriations Committee and House Commerce Sub Committees conduct separate hearings on the Bridgestone/Firestone-Ford tire recall.
September 8, 2000	Ford states in a filing with the Securities and Exchange Commission that "we have preliminarily agree to bear a portion of the costs of Firestone's recall."

The CHAIRMAN. Thank you very much, Ms. Claybrook. We will be working with you and Mr. Ditlow as we put this legislation together. Thank you. Welcome, sir.

STATEMENT OF CLARENCE DITLOW, EXECUTIVE DIRECTOR, CENTER FOR AUTO SAFETY

Mr. DITLOW. Thank you, Mr. Chairman. I ask that my entire statement be in the record. I want to touch on one aspect of the defect. And then I want to turn to the process. When the Center for Auto Safety was seeking to get the Firestone 500 recalled, the first recall was cut off at a certain date because Firestone claimed that the later made 500's had a lower failure rate and were not defective. Just as today they are claiming that the Wilderness AT has a lower failure rate and it is not defective. We continued our efforts as more and more miles accumulated on the 500's. The later made 500's were proven to have the same failure rate, just as I am sure that the Wilderness ATs will in the future.

So unless there is clear and convincing evidence, and there certainly is not that to date. In the interest of public safety, we need to recall all the ATXs and all the Wilderness ATs, regardless of size and regardless of plant.

But as the tragic toll of 88 known deaths and 250 injuries continues to climb and more information adds to the record, it becomes clearer and clearer that both Ford and Firestone knew more earlier, but failed to act until there were too many complaints, too many deaths and too many injuries to conceal Firestone tire failures on Ford Explorers from public attention.

It is not coincidental that these two companies, Ford and Firestone, have been assessed the two largest finds in NHTSA's history, $500,000 by Ms. Claybrook in 1978 against Firestone over the 500, and $425,000 in 1999 against Ford for concealing defective ignition switches that caused fires. Covering up defects to avoid recalls is profitable for manufacturers. The worst case is they get caught and pay a token fine which is more than offset by the money they save in a delayed recall. If they do not get caught and the defect never becomes public, auto companies save hundreds of millions of dollars in recall costs at the expense of public safety.

All manufacturers conceal information from NHTSA and the public. Mitsubishi concealed consumer complaints through a double record bookkeeping system. Volvo was fined for not providing dealer bulletins. Toyota was fined for concealing fuel tank defects. Honda was fined for concealing seatbelt warranty claims. Chrysler was just fined within the past few weeks $400,000 for concealing fuel system defects. GM concealed the most lethal defect in NHTSA's history, side saddle gas tanks on 1973 to 1987 pickups that burned to death over 800 people and got away without a recall.

But when it comes to concealing defects in violation of Federal and State laws, coverup is culture at Ford Motor Company. By concealing defects, Ford does profit by avoiding the cost of the recalls. Its vehicles pollute and its consumers ride at risk of highway crashes, deaths and injuries. EPA has fined Ford three times for emission violations. And one of those was a $3.5 million criminal fine when Ford kept a double set of books much as Mitsubishi did on a mission problem.

In 1999, just to show how recall pays or fine pays, in ignition switches, Ford was fined $425,000 on a failure to recall 8 million vehicles earlier. That is a nickel a vehicle. No other auto company holds such a widespread reputation for lawlessness over the years as does Ford. And I want to point out a personal example. During the 1980's, NHTSA conducted five investigations into stalling and in Ford vehicles in which Ford withheld documents which would have shown a common cause of stalling, ignition module failure. And once again, hotter states like Arizona, Southern California, Texas, had greater frequency because it was a heat related problem. Those Fords—and there are 14 million of them still on the road—have a 9-percent higher fatal crash record. Because they stall unexpectedly at any time and at any speed.

And just last week a California judge announced that he would order the recall of the Fords in California with defective ignition modules. And in the stinging indictment, Judge Ballachey found that Ford withheld responsive information from NHTSA that it was obligated to provide. It was not for Ford to decide what safety meant. But Ford fraudulently concealed vital information related to vehicle safety from the consuming public.

And I cannot help but compare what Ford President and CEO Jac Nasser has repeatedly told the American public about Firestone tires. That your safety is our top priority. And yet, when Ford was asked in California what safety was, it said it did not know. And there was no written definition of what safe is within Ford Motor Company. Any motor company that has no definition of safety has no moral compass and it is why we have crises like the Firestone tires on Ford Explorers.

Now, the case law on safety defects is very clear in establishing a per se theory of failure of any component which can lead to loss of control or mobility or fire. And it requires showing only that such a critical component failed. And there need not be any crashes, injuries or deaths, just the unreasonable risk of crashes, injuries or death. And I could not disagree more with Administrator Bailey, who is new on the job. But the very seminal and original defect case of Kelsy-Hayes wheels which started based on a single complaint. If Mrs. Bailey was correct in that they do not open cases until they get multiple complaints, we would not have the Kelsy-Hayes wheels case decided by the U.S. Court of Appeals.

Finally, the biggest single problem in the National Traffic and Motor Vehicle Safety Act is that it has no teeth if a manufacturer covers up a defect. Ford is a recidivist in covering up defects and avoiding recalls. And the best way to make Ford and other companies obey the law is to put criminal penalties into that law which the auto industry successfully lobbied against when the Safety Act was passed. Thank you.

[The prepared statement of Clarence Ditlow follows:]

PREPARED STATEMENT OF CLARENCE DITLOW, EXECUTIVE DIRECTOR, CENTER FOR AUTO SAFETY

Mr. Chairmen and members of the Committee, thank you for the opportunity to testify on the recall of Bridgestone/Firestone tires on Ford light trucks and sport utility vehicles (SUVs). I am Clarence Ditlow, Executive Director of the Center for Auto Safety (CAS) which is a non-profit organization founded by Consumers Union and Ralph Nader in 1970 but is now independent of both. The Center works to improve vehicle and highway safety and was the consumer group responsible for the recall of 19.5 million Firestone 500 steel belted radials in 1978–80.

Although there are many similarities between the Firestone 500 and the Firestone/Ford tire failures, there is a key difference—the role of the vehicle on which the tires are mounted. In the Firestone 500 recall, there were more tires and complaints (14,000 then versus 1,400 today) but fewer deaths (41 then versus 88 and rising today). The primary vehicle in which Firestone ATX, ATX II and Wilderness tire tread separations and deaths have been associated is the Ford Explorer, an SUV which has been marketed as a passenger car. Although the Explorer meets essentially the same standards as passenger cars (albeit on a delayed schedule) there are no standards on rollover and only a weak standard on roof strength for rollover protection. The Explorer is the worst kind of vehicle on which to put a bad tire. A tread separation or other tire failure can lead to a fatal rollover. A tire made for an SUV like the Explorer should have an extra margin of safety built into it like a nylon ply because the consequences of failure can be so bad.

As the tragic toll of 88 known deaths and 250 injuries continues to climb and more information is added to the public record, it becomes clearer and clearer that both Ford and Firestone knew more earlier but failed to act until there were too many complaints, deaths and injuries to conceal Firestone tire failure on Ford Explorers from public attention.

Firestone and Ford Early Knowledge Show Companies Covered Up Defect

Emerging information show that both Ford and Firestone had early knowledge of tread separation in Firestone tires on Ford Explorers and other Ford vehicles but at no point informed the NHTSA or the American public. To the contrary, the companies concealed information on the lethal combination of Firestone tires on Ford Explorers. It is not coincidental that these two companies have been assessed the two largest fines in NHTSA's history—$500,000 in 1978 against Firestone over the 500 steel belted radial and $425,000 in 1999 against Ford for concealing defective ignition switches that shorted and started fires.

Product liability lawsuits were filed in the early 1990's on Explorer rollovers caused by Firestone tire failures. Lawsuits settlements and discovery contained confidentiality agreements and document protective orders so information on tread separation on Firestone tires causing rollovers on Ford Explorers could be concealed. NHTSA began receiving consumer complaints in 1990–93 and provided Ford and Firestone with summaries of all such complaints as part of its standard policy. In 1996, Arizona state agencies confronted Firestone about tread separations, particularly in hot weather, in Firestone steel-belted radials. In 1998, Ford began receiving complaints on Firestone tire failures on Explorers in other countries. That same year, State Farm Insurance informed NHTSA that it had received 21 damage claim reports on Firestone radial failures on Ford Explorers dating back to 1992. In late 1999, Ford began to replace Firestone tires on Explorers in other countries but failed to notify NHTSA despite a Ford internal memo showing both Ford and Firestone concerned about the duty to report this to NHTSA.

Covering up defects to avoid recalls is profitable for manufacturers even if they get caught by NHTSA. The worst case is they get caught and pay a token fine which is more than offset by the money they save in a delayed recall which always has a lower completion rate. If they don't get caught by NHTSA and the defect never becomes public, auto companies save hundreds of millions of dollars in recall costs at the expense of public safety and lives.

All manufacturers, conceal information from NHTSA and the public whether it's by secrecy agreements in product liability lawsuits or by withholding information directly from NHTSA. Mitsubishi was recently caught concealing consumer complaints through a double record keeping system. Volvo was fined $17,000 this year for not providing dealer bulletins to NHTSA as required by the Vehicle Safety Act.

Volvo got caught only because one of the bulletin it withheld was on Joan Claybrook's Volvo. Toyota was fined for concealing fuel tank defects. Honda was fined for concealing seat belt warranty claims and not doing a recall until NHTSA began an investigation. Chrysler is under investigation for concealing fuel rail defects in its LH models. GM concealed the most lethal defect in NHTSA's history—side saddle gas tanks on 1973–87 pickups that burned to death over 800 people—for over 20 years through confidential settlements that virtually all the trucks were beyond the 8-year statute of limitation for mandatory recall by the time NHTSA caught up to GM. If manufacturers get beyond the 8-year limit and there is no recall, the maximum fine is $1,000 (adjusted for inflation) per withheld document. If they get caught in time to do a recall, then the maximum fine is $1,000 per vehicle or tire which should have been recalled earlier capped at $800,000 (adjusted to $925,000 for inflation). Strictly peanuts. In the case of Ford which was fined $425,000 in the 8 million vehicle ignition switch recall, the fine came to a nickel a car.

Cover Up Is a Culture at Ford Motor Company

When it comes to concealing defects and violations of federal and state laws, cover up is a culture at Ford Motor Company. By concealing defects Ford profits by avoiding costly emission and safety recalls. Its vehicles pollute and its consumers ride at risk of highway crashes, deaths and injuries. In the early 1970's the Environmental Protection Agency fined Ford twice for cheating on emission tests. In one case, the Department of Justice filed a criminal complaint against Ford that resulted in a record $7 million fine of which $3.5 million was an unprecedented criminal fine against an auto company for false reporting of emission information to the government.[1] In that case, Ford kept a double set of book with the correct one for internal use and a false one for the US government, much the same as Mitsubishi did on consumer complaints.

In the late 1970's, the Federal Trade Commission sued Ford for conducting secret warranties on engine and transmission problems.[2] In the late 1980's, Ford withheld documents from the National Highway Traffic Safety Administration during investigations on stalling in Ford vehicles to avoid recalls.[3] In 1999, NHTSA reached a settlement which required Ford to pay a $425,000 penalty for its coverup and failure to timely recall million of vehicles with defective ignition switches that set parked vehicles on fire.[4] In 1998, the Environmental Protection Agency again fined Ford, this time $7.8 million in total payments including a $3.5 million fine, for cheating emission standards by illegally installing emission control defeat devices on its vehicles.[5] No other auto company holds such a widespread reputation for lawlessness over the years. And this doesn't even consider the infamous exploding Ford Pinto which resulted in a criminal indictment against company. Even though Ford was narrowly acquitted in the Pinto criminal case, a model corporation would not come close to the edge of breaking the law.

California Court Uncovers Ford's Latest Cover Up—Stalling In 14 Million Vehicles

During the 1980's, NHTSA conducted five investigations into stalling in Ford vehicles. During those investigations, Ford withheld documents from NHTSA that would have shown a common cause of stalling—failure of the Thick Film Ignition (TFI) module mounted on the distributor when its temperature rises above 125°C and cuts out, causing the vehicle to stall on the highway. There are over 14 million vehicles still on American roads today that suffer from the same readily-correctable design defect that can cause the engine to stop abruptly and unexpectedly, at any time and at any speed, leaving the driver without power-assisted steering or brakes and the vehicle disabled. Vehicles with the distributor mounted TFI module have a 9% higher fatal crash rate than those with a different module system.

Ford Motor Company has known about this problem since it began, yet it has concealed it from consumers and government regulators for well over a decade. Just as in Firestone tires on Ford Explorers, a prime instrument in Ford's cover up is secrecy agreements in product liability lawsuits. Over 900 product liability lawsuits have been filed against Ford on these vehicles with protective orders and confidential settlement agreements entered in many.

---

[1] Department of Justice Press Release Announcing Settlement in *United States v Ford Motor Co.*, Feb. 13, 1973.

[2] In the Matter of Ford Motor Co., 96 FTC 362 (1980).

[3] Letter from Frank Seales, NHTSA Chief Counsel, to Jay D. Logel, Office of Chief Counsel, Ford Motor Co., Jan. 26, 1998.

[4] Settlement Agreement Between Ford Motor Co. & NHTSA, March 11, 1999.

[5] Department of Justice Press Release, June 8, 1998.

In a landmark decision on August 29, 2000, in *Howard v. Ford Motor Co.,* (Case No. 763785–2, Alameda County Superior Court, California State Judge Michael Ballachey announced he would order the recall of 1.8 million 1983–95 Ford vehicles in California with defective ignition modules that fail and cause dangerous stalls on highways. Judge Ballachey's ruling is the first court order of a recall in the United States outside NHTSA. In a stinging indictment of Ford Motor Co., Judge Ballachey found:

> Ford withheld responsive information from NHTSA that it was obligated to provide. [P. 5] It was not for Ford to decide what "safety" meant, or what levels of warranty returns obligated it to report to the EPA. Ford's responsibility was to respond to legitimate government inquiries with appropriate information so that an independent evaluation could determine the presence or absence of a problem. [P. 6] Ford failed to meet its obligations to report safety related defect information to relevant governmental agencies and, by so doing concealed vital information related to vehicle safety from the consuming public. This fraudulent concealment . . . constitutes a violation of both Civil Code sections 1770(a)(5) and (7). [P.8]

The problem is caused by the thick film ignition ("TFI") modules, a key ignition-system component that Ford installed in more than 22 million vehicles it manufactured and sold in the 1983 through 1995 model years. The TFI module regulates the electrical current that fires the air-fuel mixture in each of the engine's cylinders. To reduce costs, Ford installed the TFI on the distributor, one of the hottest locations under the hood. But because the TFI module is sensitive to heat, its mounting location creates an inordinate propensity for the TFI module to fail due to thermal stress. Making the problem even more insidious is its phantom nature. A TFI module can fail on an intermittent basis when hot, then function again when the engine cools, without leaving a trace of physical evidence that the TFI module had failed.

Rather than bearing the expense of moving the TFI module to a cooler location away from the engine—a solution that Ford engineers recommended to management for years—Ford decided to employ a less costly solution: to leave the module on the distributor, but make it last long enough to function during the warranty period, thereby forcing consumers to bear the cost of post-warranty failures that Ford knew would continue to occur in large numbers. As a result, over *13 million* replacement TFI modules (which are designed to last for the life of the vehicle without maintenance or repair) have been sold to consumers at a cost of nearly *$2 billion.*

Despite an extraordinary number of complaints from consumers, Ford managed to conceal the TFI problem from government regulators. From 1983 through 1989 the National Highway Traffic Safety Administration (NHTSA) conducted *five* separate investigations into stalling complaints by Ford customers. In response to these investigations, Ford concealed what it knew about the TFI problem and persuaded NHTSA to close each investigation without taking action. As a result of the class action, NHTSA opened an investigation in 1997, in which it concluded that Ford had withheld key documents during earlier investigations. By then, the 8-year statute of limitations on NHTSA's authority to order a recall had expired, preventing NHTSA from taking any meaningful enforcement action.

Ford continues to deny that TFI-related stalling causes a safety risk. According to Ford, TFI failure causes the vehicle to buck, hesitate, and experience other "driveability" symptoms that provide a warning that the TFI module is about to fail. But Ford took the exact opposite position when it attempted to excuse its failure to report to the Environmental Protection Agency and the California Air Resources Board over 1 million TFI modules (which EPA and CARB deem "emissions-related" components) that were returned under warranty. In direct contradiction to Ford's contention that TFI module failure does not pose a safety risk because TFI-induced bucking and hesitation provides plenty of warning, Ford claimed that TFI module failure cannot affect air quality because such failure occurs suddenly and without warning.

Having concealed the true nature and scope of the TFI defect from NHTSA, from EPA, and other regulatory agencies, Ford then used its bargaining power to keep secret the information about the TFI defect in the only other context in which the truth could air: private civil litigation. Given the intermittent, phantom nature of the TFI problem, few people ever discovered that TFI failure was the cause of their injuries, and even fewer sued because of it. When personal-injury plaintiffs did discover what Ford knew about the problem, Ford paid millions of dollars in settlements requiring lawyers to return hot documents, remain silent about what they learned from those documents, and refrain from assisting others in similar litigation against Ford. Just as in Firestone tires on Ford Explorers, the TFI product liability cases against Ford involve tragic injuries. In *Phan v Budget Rent a Car & Ford*

Motor Co., there were two deaths, one quadriplegic and four other injuries when a 1990 Mercury Sable stalled at highway speeds.

In the recall of Ford Explorers for Firestone tire tread separations, Ford President & CEO Jac Nasser has repeatedly told the American public that "Your Safety Is Our Top Priority." Yet in *Howard v Ford Motor Co.,* Ford told the court it didn't know what safety was. As Judge Ballachey observed after hearing the testimony of top executives including its former CEO Harold Poling, its former Vice Chairman Louis Ross and Vice Presidents Robert Transou and Helen Petrauskus among others:

> Ford's dissimulation reached its nadir in the testimony of Bob Wheaton, Ford's witness designated as most knowledgeable about safety issues when he insisted that "safe is too subjective" and denied knowledge of any "written definition of what safe is within Ford Motor Company." Other Ford executives were similarly evasive when pressed on the question of whether or not a failed TFI module, under any circumstances, presented an unreasonable risk of safety. [P. 5].

Yet the case law on safety defects is very clear in establishing a per se theory of failure of any component which can lead to loss of control or mobility or fire which requires showing only that such a critical component failed and that there need not be any crashes, injuries or deaths, just the unreasonable risk or crashes, injuries or deaths. The leading case on defects under the Vehicle Safety Act is United States v. General Motors, 518 F.2d 420 (DC Cir. 1975), which involved the recall of 200,000 GM pickups for Kelsy-Hayes wheel failures. NHTSA opened the investigation based on a report of a single failure from Ralph Nader and ultimately showed a failure rate of under 0.2%. The US Court of Appeals decision upholding the recall established the key requirements for recalls:

- Non de minimis number of failures in use which normally will not be a substantial percentage of components produced.
- Function of failure rate and severity of consequences.
- Ordinary owner abuse such as tire underinflation must be anticipated by manufacturer.
- Need not show any deaths or injuries.

Why Didn't NHTSA Learn About Firestone/Ford Earlier

Tire defects are difficult to discover because so few consumers complain about them and because existing crash data bases are not detailed enough to identify them. When CAS initiated its efforts on the Firestone 500, we received no more than 100 tire complaints per year compared to 15,000 vehicle complaints. NHTSA is no different than CAS and receives very few tire complaints compared to vehicle complaints. To compound matters, few of the consumers who do complain provide the crucial tire identification number located on the inside side wall or even the size and model of tire. CAS goes back to consumers for such information but can no longer do so in the case of complaints in NHTSA's data base because NHTSA keeps their identity confidential.

NHTSA should have opened an investigation in 1998 when State Farm provided information on the 21 claims because the agency often opens a defect investigation on as few as two complaints as this Committee has noted in the past. Rather than being low, the 21 State Farm claims is almost astronomical. NHTSA needs to cast a broader net on tire complaints because so few come into the agency and because the consequence of tire failure can be so catastrophic compared to other defects. If NHTSA doesn't have the authority to compel information on foreign recalls, then it should be given that authority by Congress.

Legislative Recommendations

The biggest single problem in the National Traffic and Motor Vehicle Safety Act is that it has no teeth if a manufacturer covers up a defect. As shown above, Ford Motor Company is a recidivist when it comes to covering up defects and avoiding recalls. The best way to make Ford and other auto and tire companies obey the law is to put criminal penalties into the law which the industry successfully lobbied against when the Safety Act was passed in 1966.

A particular dilemma with tire recalls is that a manufacturer has no obligation to replace a tire for free if it is more than 3 years old. With radial tires that last 50,000 miles or more, this limit should be repealed. If a manufacturer conceals a defect until the statutory period for free repair or replacement expires, they can get away without a recall. In cases of concealment, the statutory limit on free replacement and repair should be tolled. Moreover, the statute does not provide for reimbursement where a consumer pays for replacement or repair prior to a recall. Congress should remedy that by providing for reimbursement in the statute.

The Firestone/Ford recall of 6.5 million tires to date shows another problem in the recall system—the shortage of critical safety components such as these tires in large recalls. If parts and tires are unavailable from the recalling manufacturer, then the public rides at risk until replacements become available for their vehicles. CAS is aware of at least 5 deaths in rollover accidents involving Firestone tire tread separation on Ford Explorers since the initial recall was announced. Although Ford and Firestone have announced they would reimburse consumers who buy competitor tires, there is no guarantee they will do so. Indeed, Firestone rescinded its offer until a Kentucky court issues an order prohibiting it. The Safety Act should be amended to give NHTSA the authority to order replacement and repair from competitors where there is an imminent safety hazard and the recalling company cannot meet demand.

Since NHTSA failed to implement this Committee's recommendation in 1978 that FMVSS 109 be upgraded, Congress should amend the Safety Act to require NHTSA to upgrade not only FMVSS 109 but also FMVSS 119 with specific direction to determine whether a even more stringent tire standard should be set for SUVs with their higher rollover propensity than passenger cars. This Committee should also direct NHTSA to reassess its 1981 decision to drop its proposed rulemaking on low tire pressure warning devices.

The Safety Act should be amended to provide criminal penalties for knowing and willful violations of safety standards and refusal to recall in line with FDA and CPSC authority and in removing the ceiling on civil penalties under the Safety Act to be in line with the Clean Air Act which has no ceiling for violation of vehicle emission standards. Other needed legislative changes include:

- Repeal the statutory limit on recalls.
- Toll the statute of limitation where auto and tire companies conceal defects.
- Give NHTSA the authority to order replacement and repair from competitors where there is an imminent safety hazard and the recalling company cannot meet demand.
- Provide for reimbursement of repairs and replacements made prior to recall.
- Require NHTSA to upgrade not only FMVSS 109 but also FMVSS 119 with specific direction to determine whether an even more stringent tire standard should be set for SUVs with their higher rollover propensity than passenger cars. This Committee should also direct NHTSA to reassess its 1981 decision to drop its proposed rulemaking on low tire pressure warning devices.

These legislative recommendations are designed to prevent another public safety crisis like the Firestone tires on Ford Explorers from ever happening again. But for now, the single most important thing to be done is for Ford and Bridgestone/Firestone to recall all ATX, ATX II and Wilderness tires regardless of size and plant where made.

The CHAIRMAN. Thank you very much, Mr. Ditlow. What can U.S. corporations and NHTSA and the Congress do to improve our ability to identify a consumer safety problem sooner? It seems to me that while we may not have issues of this magnitude, quite often we are sort of like the guy following the parade. How do we get out in front on these situations more effectively?

Mr. DITLOW. Ford and Firestone are learning a terrible lesson. That when you cover up a safety problem and do not exercise leadership, it costs sales. But for the government agencies, their only way to do this is to have a stronger enforcement mechanism. Unfortunately, they have to use the bully pulpit. They have to expose these problems. But for the car companies——

The CHAIRMAN. Is it instructive, the response to Senator Hollings' questions that there has been no initiated recall in the last 5 years by NHTSA?

Mr. DITLOW. I think the auto companies over the last—not just the last 5 years, but the last 15 years, have recognized that

NHTSA is not a strong enforcer and will not go to the mat for a mandatory recall.

The CHAIRMAN. Do you share that view, Ms. Claybrook?

Ms. CLAYBROOK. I do. I think there are a number of things that NHTSA could do which include having relationships with auto repair facilities, independent auto repair shops, which we did in the 1970's, asking them to send in defective products, and working with insurance companies on a regular basis. And I think your legislation should cover, as the Secretary suggested, requirements for the companies to send NHTSA information on a regular basis. NHTSA also should get notification of lawsuits by the companies, and ask lawyers who have cases to resist protective orders or at least let the agency know that there is such a gag order. NHTSA should work with fleet owners. There are a lot of fleet owners who would be very cooperative. And state agency fleet owners, as in Arizona for example.

The CHAIRMAN. Mr. Ditlow, please continue.

Mr. DITLOW. I agree with Joan wholeheartedly. And I have detailed recommendations along those lines. And we need the cooperation of a wide sector to get defect investigations and recalls done. So I would just answer questions now.

The CHAIRMAN. Let us talk about the foreign problem again. How do we do a better job if there is a recall in Saudi Arabia of tires—well, let us use Venezuela because the argument is that they were different kinds of tires. Venezuela problems arose there. And yet, apparently neither NHTSA nor anybody else that was in a position of authority knew about it. What do you do about that situation? I will begin with you, Mr. Ditlow.

Mr. DITLOW. We have multi-national corporations who market in different countries. And with that goes an obligation to respond to report problems in foreign countries here. I mean, I think everyone now agrees that there should be reporting. But NHTSA should issue a regulation tomorrow requiring that reporting.

The CHAIRMAN. Ms. Claybrook.

Ms. CLAYBROOK. NHTSA has issued something called "The Global Agreement to Harmonize Motor Vehicle Standards" that the auto companies have been pushing for for a long time, because they want to have the ability to sell a product in any country with the same standards. But they have never issued anything for international cooperation in any formal way on enforcement and defects as they have with standards to enforcement. If the companies are going to get the benefit of the standards being harmonized, I think that they should have the obligation and responsibility to also participate in reporting defects. And this can come from the companies as well as from foreign governments, from both.

The CHAIRMAN. I want to thank both of you. We want to work with you as we develop this legislation. I want to make a caution though here to both of you who are committed public advocates. Too often, we try to make the perfect be the enemy of the good here. I think we ought to do what we can in the next several weeks and get legislation passed. And then I am committed to going back again next year and looking at additional legislation. Because we are going to have to build consensus on this if we expect to pass some important aspects of what clearly are a myriad of issues here concerning safety.

So I look forward to working with you and hope that we will be able to come up with something very important, very substantive, but with the recognition that in this relatively short period of time, we are not going to be able to do everything. Deal?

Ms. CLAYBROOK. Deal.

The CHAIRMAN. It is agreed. Thank you very much.

Ms. CLAYBROOK. So you put us on the hot seat just like the companies.

The CHAIRMAN. Thank you for being here.

[Whereupon, at 1:20 p.m., the committee was adjourned.]

APPENDIX

LETTER FROM JOHN T. LAMPE, EXECUTIVE VICE-PRESIDENT, BRIDGESTONE/FIRESTONE, INC.,

September 20, 2000.

Hon. JOHN MCCAIN,
Chairman,
Senate Commerce Committee,
Science and Transportation Subcommittee,
Washington, DC.

Hon. OLYMPIA J. SNOWE,
United State Senate,
Washington DC.

RE: HEARING ON FORD-BRIDGESTONE/FIRESTONE TIRE RECALL

Dear Chairman McCain and Senator Snowe:

At the September 12, 2000 Commerce Committee hearing, I referred to a 1996 report pertaining to tire inspections that Bridgestone/Firestone conducted at the behest of the Arizona Game and Fish Department. A copy of that report was forwarded to you on September 19, along with a second, independent tire inspection report that Bridgestone/Firestone completed on April 16, 1997.

I based my September 12 testimony on verbal reports from Bridgestone/Firestone personnel who relied on their recollection of those events. After reviewing the reports, I am writing to clarify my testimony, which regrettably contained some inaccuracies. The vast majority of the tires identified in the reports were "LT" (light truck) tires, not passenger tires as I originally believed, and the application of such LT tires in off-road conditions is not improper. I was, however, correct that a substantial majority of the tires were not the size recommended by the vehicle manufacturer for the Department's vehicles.

The Arizona inspection revealed no defects pertinent to the sizes and types of tires subject to Bridgestone/Firestone's recently announced United States recall. The recall affects passenger-sized tires, not those tires sized for light trucks. Also, the types of most tires analyzed in the Arizona reports were of the Firehawk ATX and Steeltex lines, not the Wilderness AT and Radial ATX/ATXII tires subject to recall.

I will continue to apprise you immediately of any new information related to this matter should I receive it. I remain dedicated to cooperating fully with you and your Committee.

Sincerely,

JOHN T. LAMPE,
Executive Vice-President,
Bridgestone / Firestone, Inc.

○